Spirited Leading and Learning

Peter B. Vaill

Spirited Leading and Learning

Process Wisdom for a New Age

Jossey-Bass Publishers
San Francisco

Jossey-Bass books and products are available through most bookstores. To contact Jossey-Bass directly, call (888) 378-2537, fax to (800) 605-2665, or visit our website at www.josseybass.com.

Substantial discounts on bulk quantities of Jossey-Bass books are available to corporations, professional associations, and other organizations. For details and discount information, contact the special sales department at Jossey-Bass.

Library of Congress Cataloging-in-Publication Data
Vaill, Peter B.
    Spirited leading and learning : process wisdom for a new age /
Peter B. Vaill.—1st ed.
        p.   cm.—(The Jossey-Bass business & management series)
    Includes bibliographical references and index.
    ISBN 0-7879-4327-4
    1. Leadership 2. Organizational learning. I. Title. II. Series.
HD57.7.V35   1998
658.4'092—dc21   98-24501

FIRST EDITION
HB Printing   10 9 8 7 6 5 4 3 2

The Jossey-Bass
Business & Management Series

Contents

Acknowledgments

All but two of the chapters of this book were written and/or published because of the support and encouragement of a particular individual. Along with the hundreds of colleagues and students over the years who have stimulated and shaped my thinking, I wish to thank these eight individuals in particular for their help, their occasional badgering, and their constant faith:

Chapter Two: John D. Adams
Chapter Three: W. Warner Burke
Chapter Four: Allan R. Cohen
Chapter Six: Edwin P. Hollander
Chapter Eight: Allan Drexler
Chapter Nine: Peter J. Frost
Chapter Ten: Anthony Moore
Chapter Eleven: Suresh Srivastva

Some of these chapters are very different from what these friends were expecting. I hope that the deviations are on the high side, but in any event, I am responsible for whatever deficiencies these chapters contain.

P.B.V.

*These essays are love letters
to the many students, colleagues, and practicing managers
it has been my privilege to know.*

The Author

Peter Vaill holds the Distinguished Chair in Management Education at the Graduate School of Business, University of St. Thomas, Minneapolis–St. Paul, Minnesota. He received his B.A. degree (1958) in psychology from the University of Minnesota, and his M.B.A. degree (1960) in general management and D.B.A. degree (1964) in organizational behavior from the Harvard Business School.

Vaill is known for his innovative approaches to managerial leadership and organizational behavior. His essay "Toward a Behavioral Description of High-Performing Systems" (1972) was the first contemporary description of what has come to be called "organizational excellence." He designed and taught one of the first courses in cross-cultural management offered in a U.S. management school and has pioneered in speaking and writing about the spiritual problems of managerial leaders. He is well known for his ideas about what he calls "permanent white water"—the extremely turbulent conditions in organizations and society that managerial leaders are coping with. He is a member of the Academy of Management, the Organizational Behavior Teaching Society, the National Organization Development Network, and the American Association of Higher Education and is a charter member of the NTL Institute. He has keynoted the programs of these and other professional societies many times.

Vaill has worked with many well-known corporations and with most of the major agencies of the U.S. government, as well as with many universities, health systems, and professional associations. His work has taken him to Canada, Great Britain, Germany, Belgium, Holland, Switzerland, the Scandinavian countries, Egypt, Iran, Japan, and Colombia. He has published many articles in the academic and professional literature. He is the author of a book of essays, *Managing as a Performing Art: New Ideas for a World of Chaotic Change* (1989). His new theory of managerial learning was presented in his book *Learning as a Way of Being: Strategies for Survival in a World of Permanent White Water* (1996). From 1985 to 1988 he was editor of the American Management Association's journal *Organizational Dynamics*.

Vaill was formerly professor of human systems and director of the Ph.D. program at George Washington University's School of Business and Public Management and is a former dean of that school. He has also served on the management faculties of the University of Connecticut and the University of California, Los Angeles, and was visiting professor of organizational behavior at the Stanford Business School. He was a member of the board of governors of the Center for Creative Leadership from 1990 to 1997.

Vaill's hobbies include music, jogging, and sailing. He has a daughter who is a medical social worker and the mother of two, and a son who is a jazz drummer.

Part I

Process Wisdom for a New Age

1

An Invitation to the Dance

This book is a collection of essays on managerial leadership written over a fifteen-year period between the early 1980s and the late 1990s. Some of these essays have been published before and some were not published after the occasion for which they were produced. Taken together, they present a range of perspectives on the nature of managerial leadership and on its development through education and training. A central theme of the book is that managerial leadership is a different kind of thing than much management literature makes it, and that the learning process for managerial leadership needs to be changed to meet some of the neglected dimensions.

The themes that run through these essays and merge and crisscross in various ways are as follows:

1. The proper name for what we are talking about is not management and not leadership, but "managerial leadership." The worldwide need for new ideas and changed ways of working, in the midst of extreme turbulence and rapid change, demands that we think of the activity as leadership. But unlike some kinds of leaders, the leaders this book is concerned with stay around. They work in the systems they are trying to change. They also have to *manage* these systems and keep them as stable and serviceable as possible. Since the leading and the managing cannot be separated, I will be discussing managerial leaders throughout the book.

2. Managerial leadership by its very nature is not an applied science. It is concerned with a much wider range of elements and exists in a much wider range of situations than science can begin to keep up with. Continual change further invalidates the applied science model. Finally, since managerial leaders are constantly creating, stewarding, and arbitrating values, they are engaged in matters of judgment and wisdom, not scientific distinctions. It is very unfortunate that just because a very narrow range of management problems seem to lend themselves to a quasi-scientific analysis, some have concluded that managerial leadership in general can and should be thought of as an applied science.

3. Managerial leadership is very down-to-earth and situational, and yet it has to be understood in terms of timeless themes of power and friendship and choice and responsibility and community. It is a new kind of liberal art and needs to be understood as such. That managerial leadership is a new kind of liberal art—an emergence, really, of the twentieth century—is the most exciting thing about it to me. A whole program is suggested by the realization that managerial leadership belongs among the liberal arts. This book goes some of the way toward developing the argument.

4. The learning process for managerial leadership is a much more mysterious thing than higher education and the training and development profession have made of it. Chapters Five and Six deal most directly with this idea, but it comes up in most of the other chapters, too. We are talking about an activity that is an elusive blend of thought and action, of individual and group behavior, of abstract and concrete focus, of problem solving and problem finding, of creativity and routine, of economics and humanities, of societal contribution and self-advancement. The learning process must be viewed as a lifelong concern; that is not an option—except to too many management educators, who are not presenting their subject matter as though it were going to be part of lifelong development.

5. Finally, various of these essays try to show that managerial leadership is not a secular enterprise: in a whole host of ways, it is

better understood as embodying and expressing some of our highest aspirations—aspirations that routinely extend outside of local, material projects and become expressions of the meaning of our lives. In addition to all of the other ways that managerial leadership forces us to synthesize various categories of knowledge, it forces us to rethink the boundary between the secular and the sacred, between the natural and the transcendental. The essays in this book confront this question over and over: how can we seriously talk about the governance and guidance of all of humankind's institutions without talking about the "perennial philosophy" of what it means to be human?

In general, the essays fall into four broad groupings. The first part of the book—Chapters One and Two—sound all of the major themes of the book. Part Two, consisting of Chapters Three, Four, and Five, focuses on leadership. Here I talk about what I think the managerial leader is really up to. In the third section I build on that, taking up the question of learning in three ways: Chapter Six explores the nature of learning for leadership; Chapter Seven broadens the focus to the learning challenges of adult education in general, which have to be taken more seriously if we are going to work more effectively with managerial leaders; and Chapter Eight focuses on the organization development profession in particular and discusses the kinds of learning it needs to engage in if it is to continue to be helpful to managerial leaders. The fourth section of the book deals with the spiritual aspects of managerial leadership and organizational life. These three chapters contain the reasons we cannot consider the subject to be purely a secular matter. Chapter Eleven also functions as a fitting summary of many of the main points of the book.

The Afterword, prepared especially for this volume, describes more fully what the program must be for reconceiving managerial leadership as a liberal art. This chapter offers a guiding image, deliberately phrased in an informal way, of "pushy collegiality" as a fundamental description of who we are talking about and what the nature of the work is.

These are essays, not deductions from scientific findings, nor do they propound any closed-end doctrine. They try deliberately to entertain as well as illuminate. They invite you to *dance* with a particular problem or opportunity or critique. They are *all* playful sketches in the best sense of that phrase, despite the serious tone that creeps in from time to time. Each essay is merely the start of a conversation. You might say that these essays aspire to stimulate in you not a "Yeah, but . . ." response, but rather a "How interesting, and furthermore . . ." response. We shall see if they succeed.

2

Process Wisdom for a New Age

The "process wisdom" of this chapter's title will be displayed and discussed in two ways. First, I will quote some of those whose consciousness of the nature of life is already transformed. I suggest that in getting beyond the old positivist-objectivist worldview, there is a remarkably consistent vision of the world as flow and as process in the thinking of whose who seek to understand and repair the excesses of Western thought. Second, there is process wisdom *for* the process of understanding and repairing the excesses of Western thought, particularly as such thought appears in organizational conduct. I use various behavioral scientists whose work has been memorable for working practitioners as exemplary of this process awareness. Positivist-objectivist facts and methods simply do not facilitate liberation. Many men and women are doing something other than merely communicating facts and methods. There is process wisdom in this something else.

This chapter closes with a four-element theory of what human action in organizations might look like if it were transformed by the process wisdom I discuss. This remark by the British biologist J. Z. Young perhaps captures the spirit of what is attempted here: "Why

---

Note: From J. Adams (ed.), *Transforming Work*. Alexandria, Va.: Miles River Press, 1984, pp. 17–34. Reprinted with permission.

must anyone seek for new ways of acting? The answer is that in the long run the continuity of life itself depends on the making of new experiments. . . . The continuous invention of new ways of observing is man's special secret of living" (Young, 1960, pp. 65–66).

Organizational Transformation and the Idea of a Disciplinary Matrix

Organizational transformation (OT) means change in thought and action at a much more fundamental level than has been accomplished so far by most change agents. Since Kuhn (1970), we have used the word *paradigm* to refer to the deeper organizing principles that undergird everyday action. OT very probably *is* a paradigm shift for thinking about organizations and influencing them, but what does this mean?

In "Postscript," written seven years after his original essay, Kuhn reconsidered the meaning of the idea of a paradigm. He proposed *disciplinary matrix* as a better description of the phenomenon he had in mind. He suggested that a disciplinary matrix is composed of four basic elements (Kuhn, 1970, pp. 182–187): (1) *symbolic generalization*, the ways that problems within the paradigm are posed and solved (that is, the formulations that are taken as sensible); (2) *metaphysical assumptions*, the taken-as-given beliefs about what shall be treated as real; (3) *values*, which embody the basic priorities and choices of what problems to pursue and what social ends to serve; and (4) *exemplars*, those worked-out approaches and solutions that display the whole worldview as a coherent gestalt.

Kuhn did not elaborate on his choice of the phrase "disciplinary matrix," but it connotes the notion of a frame that makes *disciplined* (that is, focused, connected, directed) thought and action possible. One has a disciplinary matrix—a paradigm—when the four elements are mutually complementary and reinforcing. Today, however, the disciplinary matrix of Western social thought and action is fragmented in virtually all directions. There is a major disconnection between symbolic generalizations and metaphysical assumptions on the one hand and values and exemplars on the other. People, in other words, have established new values and new classic demonstrations of these values (that is, exemplars) more quickly than they have spelled out the new symbolic generalizations and metaphysics that accompany their work. Furthermore, at a finer level of detail, enormous ferment exists in all four of Kuhn's categories. No discipline or school of thought is secure from the winds of revolution, due partly to new substantive discoveries about man, partly to the collapsing faith in positivistic objectivity, and partly to a refreshing, even thrilling, new interest in ethics, morality, and the spiritual nature of man.

This chapter seeks to contribute to a disciplinary matrix for OT. The idea of process wisdom touches all four of Kuhn's categories. It suggests the fruitfulness of a new approach to social change (symbolic generalization); it relocates reality between the observer and observed, rather than in one or the other (a metaphysical assumption); in so doing it calls attention to the value of *relationality* as a primary ingredient of effective action (values); and it illustrates all of this in the work of men and women who have been unusually effective in fostering OT (exemplars).

Much of what follows is not really new. These issues have been quite thoroughly explored in formal philosophy, particularly since Kant. But OT is not merely philosophy, and philosophers, with the exception of a few European existentialists and American pragmatists, have not distinguished themselves for their contributions to concrete change in institutions and people. OT does affect real institutions and real people: it wants *life* to change, it wants *society* to change, it wants people more fully to discover themselves in their lives and in their thoughts and actions. OT is a many-dimensional impulse cutting across existing institutions, roles, problem statements, and goal sets. This impulse is real for an exponentially growing number of men and women. It makes OT something beyond a new label for old problems and methods.

OT is also not new in its interest in fostering change in society and organizational life. All leaders and managers are concerned with change, and leadership and management theory reflects this. More specifically, the quasi-profession known as organization development (OD) has sought for twenty-five years to bring about change in organizations. As I will discuss below, however, much of this prior thinking is founded on a paradigm that is inappropriate to what we are beginning to learn about the process of change. This older paradigm is the one the social sciences inherited from the physical and biological sciences. It is an "applied science" approach: the belief is that truths about human beings and about organizations can be objectively established and that these findings can be applied to various problems of change. Elsewhere (Vaill, 1984), I have shown that perhaps OD teaches us something else entirely about this role that science plays in the process of change. For the moment, however, let it simply be said that we are in the midst of a transition from the older applied science paradigm to something else. This chapter gives voice to process wisdom as a major component of this new alternative. To be sure, there are schools and philosophies embodying process wisdom that are far older (for example, Lao Tsu, 6th century B.C.). So far, though, few have put philosophies of process head-to-head with the gospel according to the typical American management school and corporate training department. This chapter seeks to do precisely that.

Saying Something Useful

Recently, a close colleague at another management school sent me an essay he had written about how managers make decisions. My friend asked me for feedback on the model he had developed. In reply, I reluctantly characterized his approach as a "negative phenomenology" of managerial decision making, by which I meant that I thought he was 180 degrees off: his essay described precisely how managers don't think and don't decide. He had modeled the manager as a sophisticated information-processing "machine" who thinks in terms of decision trees, tracing out linear causes and effects and optimizing her or his objectives from among the various alternative choices. The manager's mind, in this theory, could be portrayed as a wiring diagram with circuits that opened and closed. Everything was conscious; everything was calculated.

My friend's reaction to this was to understand and, somewhat ruefully, agree to what I was saying. But then, in a final paragraph of his acknowledgment, he uttered a genuine cry of the spirit. He said, perhaps to justify his quest for a model of how managers' minds work, "I would like to think that someone, someday, could say something useful to managers."

This was hardly the first time that I had heard, or said myself, that behavioral scientists ought to "say something useful" to managers. Utility, in fact has been a dominant value in the disciplinary matrix of the American behavioral sciences for the entire twentieth century. Yet here we are in the 1980s still trying to figure out how to be relevant. My colleague's statement, and the many like it one hears so often, are really utterances of an open secret—that the American behavioral sciences don't amount to much as guides to action, that little of real value and import can be deduced from these sciences, and that little, if anything, is actually *done* as a consequence of the "knowledge" we claim to have of human behavior in organizations.

American behavioral science has been—*we* have been—saying the wrong thing. For decades we have tried to say the wrong thing better and better, for within our disciplinary matrix we have had trouble saying anything else. As long as we continue to say the wrong thing—no matter how well we say it, no matter how "reliably" and "validly," no matter how elegantly and mesmerically—it *still* will be the wrong thing. It will not feel right to the most honest ones among us, and it will not achieve any influence among practitioners.

Facts-and-Methods

This "wrong thing" American behavioral science has been saying to practitioners is what I call *facts-and-methods*. We have busily collected facts and invented methods and have then told manager-leaders that if they want to be effective they have to absorb our facts and learn our methods. In approaching our task this way, we persistently ignore three things:

1. History has seen legions of managers and leaders who were unaware of our facts and indifferent to our methods, who nonetheless have been outstanding both in getting the job done and in attending to the needs of organization members.

2. The overwhelming majority of managers and leaders, even the most dutiful and dependent, find our facts-and-methods only marginally useful and not very interesting. The most earnest and impressionable among them try to take the medicine we prescribe. The more skeptical among them think it's mostly useless, and some of the daring ones even say so out loud.

3. The best of the lot of behavioral scientists—the Maslows, Rogerses, Lewins, Mayos, Roethlisbergers, McGregors, Tannenbaums, Trists, and so many others—are influential and memorable with managers and leaders for who they *are*, not for what they *know*. It is the way they are, the way their minds work, the way they express themselves in their protean passions that we love and remember. One does not read Peter Drucker or Warren Bennis for the facts, but rather for the song of possibility that sounds through their writings. They are people whom it is worth the trouble and expense to know personally. (Each of us has our own list of "giants"; it need not be mine. The point is the same.)

The best among us are living proof that we have been saying the wrong thing, for the best among us have understood in our own ways, dim and acute, florid and dry, spare and prolix, what the enterprise is really about: the enterprise is really about what it means *to be in the world with responsibility*. In choosing this phrase to characterize the situation of manager or leader, I draw heavily on the European existentialist tradition, most notably on Martin Heidegger, who made *being-in-the-world* the fundamental fact of human existence (Heidegger, [1927] 1962). This concept captures formally what practicing managers and leaders have been saying to theorists and consultants for years: "My situation is more complex and unique than your theory allows for!" To be in an organizational world with responsibility for what happens there, to be grounded and rooted there, to be "thrown" there, as Heidegger would say, *is to be unable to select only those parts of one's world the theory deals with for attention*. This is why the facts-and-methods of so many well-intentioned behavioral scientists don't work; they are more selective than the person who is responsible for the situation can afford to be.

It is behavioral scientists' *own* ways of being in their worlds with their responsibilities that are the problem, and this problem derives from the strictures of the old paradigm, which requires them to practice a model of scientific inquiry and change that separates them from the very managers, leaders, and others whom they are trying to influence. These behavioral scientists have turned their fascination with managers' and leaders' situations into something the managers and leaders can hardly recognize. This is why I called my friend's elegant decision tree a negative phenomenology of choice: to a real chooser it would be unrecognizable as a map of the chooser's world as it is lived in.

Some of the material generated within the facts-and-methods paradigm has been marginally helpful when first articulated— ideas, for instance, about participation, about the nature of power, or about group roles, norms, and the dynamics of social systems.

But bold new formulations beget legions of adherents, markets for consultants, publication opportunities (and publish or perish systems!), new courses and fields of specialization. The great juggernaut of academic distinction making grinds forward, increasingly without reference to the holistic, existential predicaments of practitioners, and ends in sterility. This is the history of OD, of participative management, of group dynamics, of Theory X and Theory Y, of leadership theory. Will it be the history of the "quality of work life" movement, of the stress management movement, of the women's movement, as these are applied in academic programs and in manager-leader training and development? I think it will be. The signs are already there. Those who seek distinction by making distinctions tend to forget that being-in-the-world-with-responsibility is not well captured in two-by-two diagrams and in lists of "key" factors. With tongue only partly in cheek I recently predicted that if behavioral scientists were to try to write cookbooks, they would produce material that cooks could not read (Vaill, 1979).

Now, of course it can be argued that these remarks are far too cavalier about the facts and methods of the behavioral sciences. A serious scientist who adhered to the objectivist paradigm would be obligated to argue this way. Yet, as Kuhn said, when the paradigm shifts, many things that the old paradigm could deal with quite well are not addressed at all in the new paradigm (Kuhn, 1970, pp. 109–110). A new paradigm's great power is that it deals with issues on what is experienced as the leading edge. It deals with the issues and anomalies that matter. The facts-and-methods of modern behavioral science don't deal with the things that matter to more and more people in action roles today. Ethics matter. Feelings matter. Community matters. The human spirit matters more and more as the terrible consequences of our century's fascination with technology, exploitation, and destruction become more crushingly manifest.

Toward a Developed Alternative

In his chapter, "Revolutions as Changes of World View" (Kuhn, 1970), Kuhn himself examines the adequacy of a purely objectivist science, that is, a science that assumes that its task is to uncover the laws that govern a world conceived as real, separate, and apart from man-the-perceiver. After puzzling for several pages over the meaning of all the psychological research showing the interconnectedness of observer and observed in *all* the sciences, he expresses doubt over whether indeed there can be observer-independent truth— whether, in the language I have been using, there can be facts-and-methods that stand purely by themselves as tools for use by practitioners. Then he comes to the nub of his problem, the problem of every scientist who pays close attention to the way a process of inquiry proceeds. On first reading, the following statement sounds like a "remark," but the more I reflect on this thought of Kuhn's, the more it seems to be a cosmic cry:

> But is sensory experience fixed and neutral? Are theories simply man-made interpretations of given data? The epistemological viewpoint that has most often guided Western philosophy for three centuries dictates an immediate and unequivocal, Yes! In the absence of a developed alternative, I find it impossible to relinquish entirely that viewpoint, yet it no longer functions effectively, and the attempts to make it do so through the introduction of a neutral language of observations now seem to me hopeless [p. 126].

Now, over twenty years later, Kuhn's "developed alternative" still beckons to us. The OT movement is a profound impulse toward a developed alternative, toward ways of knowing and acting that do not misplace truth as "out there" in Kuhn's "fixed and neutral" facts-and-methods.

Writing at about the same time, the British philosopher Owen Barfield captured epigrammatically the spirit of what Kuhn was looking for. The remarkable thing about Barfield's observation is that it embodies a truth that every action taker in the social world knows: "Penetration to the meaning of a thing or a process, as distinct from the ability to describe it exactly, involves a participation by the knower in the known" (Barfield, 1961, p. 288).

The manager-leader is concerned with *meaning*, not just with pseudo-objective truth, for it is in meaning that one's being-in-the-world-with-responsibility is discovered. (Significantly, too, a recent interpretation of the *meaning* of modern physics makes substantial use of Barfield's philosophy; see Jones, 1983.)

To talk of "transformation" is to attempt to talk of the new dilemmas, predicaments, challenges, and opportunities that practicing managers and leaders have been facing since World War II. Many writers have commented on the surprising emergence of these new challenges to action. Eric Trist was one of the earliest and most penetrating of these. He spoke of the "structural presence of postindustrial society" (Trist, 1970, p. 78), by which he meant all the conditions that have rendered the facts-and-methods of orthodox, old-paradigm behavioral science obsolete. The new patterns and ambiguities of postindustrial society are too messy for old-paradigm behavioral science.

Sometimes artists catch the texture of experience long in advance of more pedestrian thinkers. In *Lord Hornblower*, C. S. Forester (n.d., p. 259) had this to say about action in complex and turbulent systems:

> War was as unlike spherical trigonometry as anything could be, thought Hornblower, grinning at the inconsequence of his thoughts. Often one approached a problem in war without knowing what it was one wanted to achieve, to prove or construct, and without even knowing fully what means were available for doing it. War was

generally a matter of slipshod, makeshift, hit-or-miss extemporization. Even if it were not murderous and wasteful it would still be no trade for a man who enjoyed logic.

Although this statement flies in the face of all mainstream leadership and management theories, I think its content and spirit correctly capture the situation of the modern executive. It says, "Goodnight, sweet paradigm of reason that detaches observer from observed and makes of meaning a subjective whim." The action trades of OT are not for those who enjoy the mechanistic, hypothetico-deductive logic of the old paradigm. Leadership in social systems is not chess, and it is not programming. It is not PERT (Project Evaluation and Review Technique) charting, and it is not systems analysis. It is not the mapping of contingencies, and it is not intellectualizing about the situational nature of one's "situation."

D. H. Lawrence, I believe, had it exactly right:

> If we think about it, we find that our life consists in this achieving of a pure relationship between ourselves and the living universe about us. This is how I 'save my soul' by accomplishing a pure relationship between me and another person, me and other people, me and a nation, me and a race of men, me and animals, me and the trees or flowers, me and the earth, me and the skies and sun and stars, me and the moon: an infinity of pure relationships, big and little, like the stars of the sky: that makes our eternity, for each one of us, me and the timber I am sawing, the lines of force I follow; me and the dough I knead for bread, me and the very motion with which I write, me and the bit of gold I have got. This, if we knew it, is our life and our eternity: the subtle, perfected relation between me and my whole circumambient universe [Lawrence, (1925) 1968, p. 528].

To those who might observe that such a thought as Lawrence's is nothing but open systems thinking in lyrical clothes, I respond, ". . . and that is all the difference." Yes, open systems ideas try to capture the dynamic nature of systems, but in scientizing the phenomenon we have killed it. Lawrence's lyricism is *part* of the idea, not just an appendage. Lawrence's thought both talks about Barfield's knower-participating-in-the-known and displays it at the same time.

The Blind Men and the Elephant in Motion ✓

The relationality of all experience contains challenges to our understanding of organizations that we have barely begun to come to terms with. I can illustrate this by extending the metaphor of the blind men and the elephant. In its conventional telling, each blind man had a grip on a different part of the beast, and they were unable to agree on what it was really, *really* like, that is, as one of Kuhn's "fixed and neutral experiences." But there is more, for the elephant isn't just standing there but instead ambles through the forest and the veldt. The blind men are trying to understand the system as it evolves and as their experience of it unfolds. The blind man clinging to a leg experiences an elliptical forward motion. He who has the misfortune to have hold of the tail is jerked and whipped about in a random fashion. A few feet forward, his colleague, in the crotch, is periodically flooded and/or pasted with output that seems to have nothing to do with the beast's motion or with the feel of the surface clung to. At the front end, another observer rides the probing trunk, jerked and whipped like the tail man but, it seems to him, in a somehow "purposeful" manner. Clinging high up on the massive haunch is another perceiver, subjected to none of the motions or indignities of his fellows and wondering what their gasps and protestations are all about. And the observer who is astride the massive neck, an accidental mahout, finds that the flexings and shifting of his *own* body seem to correlate with the gait and momentum of the beast. This leads him to think he is *steering* it and thus is uniquely qualified to say what it really, *really* is. And we with sight—what of us? Is sight in the metaphor an analogue to science in real life? Is our experience different from each blind man's? Yes. Does it replace each blind man's? No. Are we the captives of our standpoint fully as much as each blind man? Yes.

What an instructive metaphor—the blind men and the elephant! One hundred years' worth of organization theories have yet to declare the simple truth that every action taker understands: an organization is a place where everybody is right and everybody is wrong. *Everybody*. The best among us whom I mentioned a moment ago have helped action takers recognize this truth. They have done it in the way they *are*, in D. H. Lawrence's sense: not in their *findings*, but in their ways of *looking*.

If we want to help the action taker, we have to talk about what the action taker is interested in (Vaill, 1979). He or she is interested in effectively performing a set of relationships. What I have called being-in-the-world-with-responsibility in fact provides a huge agenda of puzzling relationships for us all, theorists and practitioners alike, to think about and experiment with. We have to learn about Lawrence's relationality as it appears in thinking and feeling and judging and valuing and deciding and committing and perceiving—most of all in perceiving. Notice that I have phrased all of these as gerunds, processes of action. They are not the static categories of management and leadership and change, but instead are about manag*ing*, lead*ing*, chang*ing* (Vaill, 1979, p. 3).

As open processes flowing in time, these phenomena do *not* obey the behavioral science theories and laws that derive from the old paradigm's search for Kuhn's "fixed and neutral" facts. Old-paradigm science is about the general case. Action and being-in-the-world-with-responsibility are never about the general case. They are always about specific people, specific issues, specific opportunities. As such, the practitioner has to *include* all the "other things being equal" that old-paradigm science must leave out in order to positively declare its theories and laws. Early apostles of transformation, with their insistence on coming to terms with the here and now, were right—perhaps more right than they knew. Their only error was to apply this insight only to face-to-face interpersonal relationships, when in fact it extends to everything the manager or leader is trying to deal with.

Media-Ease and Secret Paths

How much does our thinking have to change in order for us to grasp better, and help practitioners to grasp better, the nature of the transformations they are immersed in? The answer, paradoxically, is that our thinking needs to change a *lot* but in another sense not so much as we might think. It is a *shift* in thinking that is involved. The process has already started, if we consider all the yearnings and impulses and tentative forays toward ways of thinking about people and organizations that amplify and celebrate and enshrine the flowing, relational quality of existence. This new, relational thinking we find in the OT movement is still on the margins of awareness, still not quite articulate as a worldview, still not a "developed alternative" (Kuhn, 1970).

The variety of our ways of knowing obscures these relational threads. Some of us know through foursquare explication, some through parable and poetry. Many of us know through movement and other nonverbal expressions of our awareness. In the OT movement, we find more "media-ease" than in most other places in society, and this mirrors what always has been true of the best practitioners: "media-ease" is the capacity to absorb and express one's experience through a variety of media—media that involve both the left and right hemispheres of the brain and the limbic and reptilian levels as well as the neocortical. Media-ease is comfort and pleasure with the variety of windows we are endowed with as people. The old paradigm says that knowledge and truth are learned and expressed through the verbal, linear-logical windows alone. Everything else is "style" and as such is too unique for scientific laws to encompass. The new paradigm knows something different: the experience of being-in-the-world-with-responsibility and actions on behalf of one's existence—"effectiveness," if you will—depend on media-ease. At the point of action, the artificial split between true knowledge and style dissolves.

These best thinkers among us who have touched managers and leaders with their lookings rather than their findings have media-ease, almost without exception. That is why practitioners find them so approachable and so interesting as people, and so helpful in transforming understanding. These best among us walk what have been secret paths to meaning—secret in the sense that the true nature of their paths of knowing and acting could not be displayed and discussed within the confines of the old objectivist paradigm of inquiry and knowledge. Even such geniuses as Carl Rogers and Abraham Maslow bowed to the prevailing worldview from time to time and tried to make systematic, objective statements of their theories and "findings." But their dominant modes have been much more undiscussable: Rogers's insistence on the to-me-ness of his patients' experience and of his experience of his patients (1961, pp. 66–69); Lewin's realization that understanding something comes from entering into its flow and process (Marrow, 1969, p. 235); Roethlisberger's emphasis on the skills of the practitioner as *being* relational, communicative skills, and what this means for the relational communicative abilities of those who would be helpful *to* practitioners (Roethlisberger, 1968, pp. 191–192, 208–216); and Maslow's willingness, perhaps more than any other inquirer, to share his awareness of the phenomena without feeling that he must scientize himself (Maslow, 1954).

A moment ago I said that perceiving is something we need to understand in relational terms. Here is Maslow's call on that subject:

> Perception is too much the study of mistakes, distortions, illusions, and the like. . . . Why not add to it the study of intuition, of subliminal perception, of unconscious perception? Why not the study of good taste enter here?

Of the genuine, of the true, and the beautiful? How about aesthetic perception? Why do some people perceive beauty and others not? Under this same heading of perception we may also include the constructive manipulation of reality by hope, dreams, imagination, inventiveness, organizing, and ordering [Maslow, 1954, p. 365].

The answer to all these questions, of course, has been that these phenomena are too esoteric and ethereal to be reduced to the investigatory strictures of the objectivist model of inquiry. Yet we *know* these phenomena, else how could we understand Maslow's questions?! There is nothing strange about any of these phenomena to those who walk the secret paths of meaning. Maslow continues:

Unmotivated, disinterested, unselfish, perception. Appreciation. Awe. Admiration.

Plenty of studies of stereotypes, but practically no study of fresh, concrete, Bergsonian reality. Free-floating attention of the type Freud spoke about.

What are the factors that make it possible for healthy people to perceive reality more efficiently, to predict the future more accurately, to perceive more easily what people are really like, that makes it possible for them to endure or to enjoy the unknown, the unstructured and ambiguous, and the mysterious?

Why do the wishes and hopes of healthy people have so little power to distort their perceptions?

The healthier people are, the more their capacities are interrelated [Maslow, 1954, pp. 365–366].

Here was a serious person talking about what 1950s American psychology considered paradigmatic nonsense. Who could be interested in the study of, say, "awe"? Where is the intellectual and employment market for that focus? Never mind that any leader worth his or her salt would like to know more about it, would like to know how to excite it in others. It is just too loose an idea for disciplined inquiry. And to try to become disciplined about it in terms of the objectivist paradigm turns it into something else entirely, something that most practitioners find uninteresting and irrelevant. We may say the same of other phenomena that practitioners really care about—love, trust, power, leadership, change, goals and objectives, personality, motivation. Consciousness of being-in-the-world-with-responsibility has these phenomena one way; objectivist science turns them into something else.

Process Wisdom and the Developed Alternative

In the Kuhn passage quoted earlier, he spoke of "the absence of a developed alternative." This chapter has been trying to show that we are closer, perhaps, to a developed alternative, for the behavioral sciences at least, than is generally realized. There *are* symbolic generalizations, metaphysical assumptions, values, and exemplars avail-able that constitute a new disciplinary matrix (paradigm) by Kuhn's definition. We *can* avoid turning the phenomena of our experience into something unrecognizable in the name of valid truth. We *can* stop invalidating our *selves*.

I do not know exactly what the developed alternative will be, but I suggest that we all have intuitions of its nature. There are truths beyond the mechanistic, empirical truths of the paradigm that has ruled our minds for Kuhn's three centuries. We phrase them differently, separating ourselves from each other with terminology, and we value them differently, seeking distinction with distinctions. But across the wider spectrum of experience, we know what some of these truths are. Those men and women who are trying to envision what transformation is have as good a chance as any of articulating these deeper themes.

The themes are at least four in number, which together are beginning to comprise a developed alternative. The first is existence, the second is openness and relationality, the third is the nature of consciousness itself, and the fourth is spirituality. The old paradigm of objectivist science ignores all four and declares them specious when their relevance is asserted. This is why the developed alternative will be a new fundamental paradigm, rather than just a slight modification or enrichment of the traditional view.

Existence

The difference I have in mind here was eloquently captured by novelist John Steinbeck in a quotation given to me by my colleague, Karl Weick:

> The Mexican sierra has 17 plus 15 plus 9 spines in the dorsal fin. These can be easily counted. But if the sierra strikes hard on the line so that our hands are burned, if the fish sounds and nearly escapes and finally comes in over the rail, his colors pulsing and his tail beating the air, a whole new relational externality has come into being—an entity which is more than the sum of the fish plus the fisherman. The only way to count the spines of the sierra unaffected by this second relational reality is to sit in a laboratory, open an evil smelling jar, remove a still colorless fish from the formalin solution, count the spines, and write the truth. . . . There you have recorded a reality which cannot be assailed—probably the least important reality concerning either the fish or yourself.
>
> It is good to know what you are doing. The man with his pickled fish has set down one truth and recorded in his experience many lies. The fish is not that color, that texture, that dead, nor does he smell that way [Steinbeck and Ricketts, 1971, pp. 2–3].

Managers and leaders are not fish, and theorists and facilitators are not anglers. Each of them is infinitely more complex, as is their relationship. The developed alternative must face the *existence* of the practitioner. We must stop retreating into the lab, whether the real lab of the controlled experiment or the metaphorical lab of casual abstraction and categorization. We have been recording least important truths and we *must* stop.

Elsewhere (Vaill, 1974), I have developed the idea that management is a performing art. This simple metaphor brings in many of the themes I have touched on already in this chapter: that we are talking about personal expressiveness; that we are talking about a dynamic, holistic phenomenon not easily or fruitfully broken into elements and lists of key factors; and that the process of understanding such a phenomenon and the process of improving the effectiveness of those who practice it cannot be a matter of objectivist science. being-in-the-world-with-responsibility is performed expressively. With such a view we will not forget the textures and subtleties of the practitioner's existence.

Openness and Relationality

The developed alternative also will celebrate the openness that is so profoundly displayed in the preceding quote from D. H. Lawrence. That remark is truly an archetype of the new view discussed here. The statement has a crucial implication that I have never seen spelled out before. The "infinity of pure relationships" Lawrence would have us accomplish means that people are not and cannot be finished phenomena. They are creators of phenomena, not repetitive enactors of gene-driven patterns or the conditioned subjects of cultural "laws." The study of human beings cannot be the objectivist search for laws that presumably underlie the variety of human actions. What underlies human action is a variety *generator*, namely human beings! The study of human beings and the process of helping specific persons to act effectively is more a process of discovery of the new, the unanticipated, and the unprecedented than it is the application of known laws to an already-explored territory.

As Cox observed: "What you mean is never what anyone else means exactly. And the only thing that makes you more than a drop in the common bucket, a particle of sand in the universal hourglass, is the interplay of your specialness with your commonness" (Cox, 1962, p. 19). This from an essay for aspiring writers, a point of view that masks as advice but is really a description of the way we *all* are anyway: an interplay of specialness and commonness. How could anyone ever think that a "science" in its traditional, objectivist sense could be fashioned about such a creature? The facts-and-methods of American behavioral science deal only with commonness. What of specialness? That is what, in power and beauty, confronts every leader or manager who would get things done through people. Perhaps, indeed, this is the nub of the difference: the objectivist scientist searches for laws that apply commonly. The practitioner, deeply aware of her or his own specialness, always confronts others who are deeply aware of their specialness. The cynic would say that the sense of specialness is merely self-serving, that people are much more alike than they are different. But sotto voce with all such claims one hears, ". . . except of course for me."

Consciousness

The developed alternative also has to take consciousness into account. Human consciousness connects itself to the world outside it; that is its essence. The technical term is "intentionality," that is, that consciousness is consciousness *of* something. Consciousness is not a biochemical characteristic of the brain, not a set of looping circuits that merely go round and round within the skull. Consciousness is out *there* in existence in the world. It is the bridge between the biochemistry of the brain and the phenomena outside it.

To deal consciously with consciousness, a developed alternative faces perhaps its greatest challenge. To be conscious of consciousness is to free oneself from stricture—from routines, from methodologies, and from (favorite term in the old paradigm) protocols.

Those best among us who walk what I called a secret path have done this in their own ways. They have been able to let themselves be free enough to gaze at organizational life and at a manager-leader's efforts to influence it, relatively unconstrained by notions of right-theory, right-method, right-data, right-mode-of-expression of learnings, and . . . Eureka! Manager-leaders have responded enthusiastically, "Here at last is someone who is interested in my world." How can this freedom from stricture and dogma, this capacity to be conscious of one's inspection of other consciousnesses, be institutionalized in a developed alternative?

The answer lies partly in what has been called *humanism,* partly in what has been called the *artistic consciousness.* The answer also partly lies in new territory, because art and humanism, old and rich and gorgeous as they may be as modes of illuminating the human spirit, have not yet captured the idea of being-in-the-world-with-responsibility. There is an edge or dimension that seems to elude even the richest representations of how things are for us in the world, whether a Russian novel or a Shakespearean play. Lest I be accused of suggesting archly that Shakespeare or Tolstoy did not have it quite right, this is not my intent. Rather, my point is that the manifestations of being-in-the-world-with-responsibility are ever-new, and that were Shakespeare or Tolstoy alive today, neither would be concluding that there is nothing more to say. The trouble is that objectivist science is saying precisely that: the phenomena are known and fixed, and the task now is to proceed with the categorizing and the counting.

What is important about art and humanism is not what they have said but what they have attempted. Our specialness right here, right now, is the sense that is most with each of us. Documentations of what this sense has been in the past are not this sense now. We frequently feel the uniqueness of the situation we are presently immersed in. But existentially, is this the unspeakable, the unnameable? Even if it is, the least the developed alternative can do is declare the reality of this sense and not banish it as metaphysical hogwash as its objectivist ancestor has been doing. The old paradigm is awash in reductionism: "This phenomenon is nothing but a case of . . ." The opposite of reductionism is what the developed alternative must embrace: "This phenomenon is more than I can possibly know." That is the essential starting assumption.

Spirituality

Finally, it seems to me that a developed alternative has to come to terms with the spiritual. Spirituality is an aspect of our existence that is truly undiscussable in objectivist science. But why do so many men and women in positions of responsibility go to church and otherwise ponder the depths of the circumstances they find themselves in? The old paradigm does not permit them to talk about this. What goes on in their heads as they read the ancient texts, sing the ancient hymns, utter the ancient prayers?

Over a century and a half ago, Ralph Waldo Emerson spoke of the conflict between the material and the spiritual:

> You will hear everyday the maxims of a low prudence. You will hear that the first duty is to get land and money, place and name. "What is this Truth you seek? What is this Beauty?" men will ask, with derision. If, nevertheless, God has called any of you to explore truth and beauty, be bold, be firm, be true. When you shall say, "As others do, so will I. I renounce, I am sorry for it, my early visions; I must eat the good of the land, and let learning and romantic expectations go, until a more convenient season;"—then dies the man in you; then once more perish the buds of art, and poetry, and science, as they have died already in a thousand thousand men [Emerson, (1838) 1971, p. 99].

"Then dies the man [person] in you" if you deny the spirit. "Then dies the man [person] in you" if you let objectivist science control your thought and action. If you are called by something beyond what you know materially, whatever you call it and whatever you conceive it to be, respond.

Again we are in a realm that managers and leaders know almost instinctively. We are in the realm of the loneliness of command. We are in the realm of "you can't please everybody." We are in the realm of such ordinary qualities as patience, giving another chance, thanking, and taking care of each other.

I think William Barrett was right. In *The Illusion of Technique* (1978), he came, painfully and reluctantly, to the conclusion that every exercise of what he calls "the moral will" depends on a faith that is, at bottom, supernatural. Every time we say what ought to be, every time we value this over that, our choice traces back to an implicit vision of an order and a moral scheme that lies outside material existence. Somehow, we just know that what we are doing is the right thing to do.

Many of us skillfully evade this intuition. We would prefer to believe that our choices can be defended by referring to facts and validated theories right here on earth, that we do not need any revelations to anchor our truths. But Barrett, I think, is more profound. We cannot prove the rightness of our moral choices solely by appealing to the facts, methods, and theories of our material existence. We reach a point where we have run out of arguments for what we believe; they all have been refuted and shown to be shallow and ill founded. Yet we still believe what we believe. We may change what we believe over time, but the process is one of reflection and development occurring outside the boundaries of purely rational analysis.

In an earlier work, Barrett said, "Man is the measure of all things, runs an old humanist aphorism. But in fact men do not always like to assume this lonely and arrogant role of a measuring stick for all reality. Man is void and empty unless he finds something by which to measure his own Being" (Barrett, 1972, p. 137). What we mean by spirituality is consciousness' attempt to get beyond the lonely and arrogant role that Barrett spoke of. It is our name for what is missing in us; it is the object of our faith, whether that faith be in terms of a well-worked-out organized religion or in terms of something more personal and perhaps unique. This yearning we all feel, in one way or another, brings spirit back into the developed alternative. But how are we to deal with it and with the funny feelings many of us have, as products of a very secularized world, about taking it seriously once again? OT as practiced in the developed alternative will not be a secular science—that much is clear. But what will it be?

Once again, the seeds of an answer are already around us. Many of the best among us, whose ways of looking and ways of being have touched manager-leaders, are men and women of deep compassion and faith. They do not try to make their ideas the measure of all reality in Barrett's sense, and thus they are not seen by others as possessing the answer. We walk paths of understanding with them; their thinking and actions open a way for us, and *that* is why they speak so powerfully to those who are being-in-the-world-with-responsibility.

Summary

OT is a set of ideas and actions that take us beyond the nature of our existing institutions and beyond ways of thinking that support them. There is little agreement on exactly what OT is, nor should there be. As a liberating spirit in American thought its essence is multidirectional and multidisciplinary.

Major use has been made of Thomas Kuhn's phrase "a developed alternative" to refer to the fashioning of new ways of thinking about what organizations are and about the roles and needs of the men and women who inhabit them. It has been suggested that the basic characteristic of managing and leading is what I call being-in-the-world-with-responsibility. It is a phenomenon that is deeply experienced but that has been left almost wholly unaddressed by mainstream behavioral science, with its objectivist criteria for truth and relevance.

Still, there have been men and women in this century whose thought and being have touched men and women of action. In this occurrence lie some major clues to what the developed alternative of OT might be like. Four such clues are briefly described: (1) a grounding in the actual existence that is life in organizations; (2) a comfort in and enjoyment of the openness of the human spirit to D. H. Lawrence's "circumambient universe" and the absence of an impulse to close off, to limit, to categorize fixedly; (3) an understanding of human consciousness as our bridge to the world, not a radical subjectivity in which everything is relative but a locating of awareness in the relationality of human beings to the people and the things around them; and (4) a new appreciation of the spiritual nature of man and a determination to keep it *in* any new formulation of the nature of organizational life.

Part II

Leading

3

The Purposing of
High-Performing Systems

W hat brought my thinking about the purposing of high-performing systems to a head was the front page of *The Washington Post* for October 29, 1980, which carried the following headlines:

Poland's Trade Unions Set a Deadline for New Strike

The War and Peace Debate—Carter and Reagan Trade Salvos

"Landmark" FCC Ruling Allows AT&T to Enter Computer Field

1 Man Convicted in Miami Rioting

Khomeini Silent on Hostages in Speech

Ford Loss 2nd Highest in U.S. History

Aristotle and Machiavelli Get Rockville Teacher in Trouble

Lottery Company Starts $80,000 Blitz in District

Saudis Sever Ties with Libya, Cite Qaddafi Attacks

Iran Crisis Finally Forces Itself on Vance (Fifth of a Series on "The Fall of the Shah")

Note: Reprinted by permission of the publisher, from ORGANIZATIONAL DYNAMICS AUTUMN 1982. American Management Association, New York. All rights reserved.

These headlines, plus a two-column, eight-inch-high picture of the planet Saturn as photographed by the *Voyager I* spacecraft, stimulated my thinking about this page as a kind of collage.

Saturn! The picture was thrilling to me.

Already jostling my self-image was the story of the Rockville teacher who had been ordered to stop teaching Aristotle's *Poetics* and Machiavelli's *The Prince* because they were considered too difficult for his tenth-grade students; the story of Lech Walesa and his union, Solidarity, challenging the power politics in a totalitarian state; and the stories of two great American corporations, AT&T and Ford, whose fortunes and names, in another value system, have as much meaning for me as Saturn: the one losing big, the other winning big—or so it seemed. The politicians' voices provided a counterpoint in the collage. Do these guys know anything? asked a part of me.

As I reflected on what had become for me much more than just another day's front page, I felt that the *Post* editors had posed a kind of global conundrum: "Here is the nature of the world," they may have been saying, "the present and the future. You figure it out." This chapter is my attempt to be responsive, to say something new about the conundrum.

Two broad streams of thought that I had been pursuing for some nine years also affected my reflections. The first was the study of *high-performing systems* (HPSs), a phrase I use to refer to human systems that perform at levels of excellence far beyond those of comparable systems. The second focus was on what is called, in the literature, *strategic planning*. My initial inquiries into this field had depended heavily on other people's concepts and other people's data, but by the fall of 1980 I had developed my own perspectives, theories, and ways of talking about the subject.

My particular angle of vision showed me excellence written all over that front page: the achievements of *Voyager*, the struggles of Solidarity, the lonely classics teacher, the Federal Communications Commission attempting to peer competently into the murky ball of its regulatory responsibility, the single-mindedness of Qaddafi and of a Washington lottery chieftain, even the crafted vacuousness of the presidential debates. The page is testimony to the personal energy and purposefulness of men and women. My research into HPSs helped me to see how excellence and the drive to achieve it were manifesting themselves in these stories. My interest in strategic planning permitted me to see decisions that affected the survival and development of whole organizations and of the worlds in which they exist. I could also see efforts to recover from strategic blunders of the past—in, for example, the stories about Ford, Miami, the Shah, and the Polish government. Today's news often occurs because someone did something or failed to do something at the strategic level months or even years ago.

This chapter will not try to explain these particular trends and events, but it does develop a way of thinking about leadership in HPSs that applies, I think, to large-scale movements like these as well as to more mundane management situations. *The thesis of this chapter is that the definition and clarification of purposes is both a fundamental step in effective strategic management and a prominent feature of every high-performing system I have ever investigated.* This is the kernel I take from the *Post*'s collage: it shows us the ebb and flow, the basic interaction, of purposes. We have to understand this process. It is the basis of the theory I will develop in this chapter.

What Is a High-Performing System?

Because the theory of leadership developed here derives from my studies of HPSs, it is necessary at the outset to describe these systems. This section describes criteria by which I identify HPSs, and the next gives eight broad findings about HPS characteristics.

A variety of sources provided the data from which my ideas have been developed since my original formulation of the idea of an HPS in 1972 (Vaill, 1978). I have used a variety of published case studies in developing my ideas. (For example, see works by Copeland, 1958; Hunt, 1953; Kroc, 1977; and Mailer, 1970.) In addition, I have had the benefit of a number of unpublished case studies passed along to me by friends and students. These include studies of a top college marching band and a Coast Guard cutter that went from a bottom to a top rating in six months; several studies of hospital emergency rooms and shock-trauma units; various accounts of military units, both in battle and behind the lines; a study of a highly successful drug rehabilitation agency; a study of one of Washington's most successful stock brokerages; various accounts of the formation of successful small businesses; and a very large number of singular observations of excellence in one type of human system or another.

An "excellent human system"—a high-performing system—presents us at the outset with a profound conceptual problem: how does one define *excellent?* Your HPS might be my "case of the compulsive pursuit of a socially useless objective." Or vice versa. There is no real escape from this problem because the way that we define *performance* and *excellence* depends on values. As a working rule of thumb, I have treated as HPSs those organizations or groups that meet one or more of the following criteria:

1. They are performing excellently against a known external standard. The clearest example is a team that does more of something, such as manufacturing automobiles, in a given time period, or does a set amount faster than it is usually done or than it is done by the team's competitors.

2. They are performing excellently against what is assumed to be their potential level of performance.

3. They are performing excellently in relation to where they were at some earlier point in time. (This is a developmental criterion.)

4. They are judged by informed observers to be doing substantially better qualitatively than other comparable systems.

5. They are doing whatever they do with significantly fewer resources than it is assumed are needed to do what they do.

6. They are perceived as exemplars of the way to do whatever they do, and thus they become a source of ideas and inspiration for others. (This is a style criterion.)

7. They are perceived to fulfill at a high level the ideals for the culture within which they exist—that is, they have "nobility."

8. They are the only organizations that have been able to do what they do at all, even though it might seem that what they do is not that difficult or mysterious a thing.

One of the delightful things about searching for HPSs is that we discover a very large number of human systems that meet several of these criteria. Even though the behavioral sciences don't acknowledge it, excellence is alive and well. Some such organizations are famous, glamorous, or "trendy," but others are very humble and insignificant, even drab. These criteria lead us to discover many varieties of beauty in human relationships and many forms of striving that a "tighter" set of criteria would overlook. Whether we are doing serious social research or just living in the world, these criteria will introduce us to extraordinary human phenomena.

The Characteristics of High-Performing Systems

Here is what I have found out about HPSs:

1. HPSs are clear on their broad purposes and on nearer-term objectives for fulfilling these purposes. They know why they exist and what they are trying to do. Members have pictures in their heads that are strikingly congruent.

2. Commitment to these purposes is never perfunctory, although it is often expressed laconically. Motivation, as usually conceived, is always high. More important than energy level, however, is

energy focus. Motivation is "peculiar" in the literal sense of that word: "belonging exclusively to one person or group; special; distinctive; different." Credit for suggesting the term "peculiar" here goes to Deborah D. Vaill, thus ending what had been a frustrating search for the right term. (Outsiders find motivation peculiar, too, in the more usual sense of "weird, eccentric.") Energy is invested in particulars—in specific methods, tools, idea systems, arrangements, and styles.

In most HPSs, there is some sense of the operation analogous to a feeling of rhythm. One of the important peculiarities of motivation is the way members express their energy and commitment through getting into a "groove" of some kind.

3. Teamwork in HPSs is focused on the task. Social psychology's favorite distinction between task functions and group maintenance functions tends to dissolve. Members will have discovered those aspects of system operations that require integrated actions and will have developed behaviors and attitudes that fulfill these requirements.

Coupled with the previous proposition about the focus of motivation, this means that a strong conservatism is usually evident in the HPS. There are firm beliefs in a "right organizational form," and a noticeable amount of effort is devoted to attaining and maintaining this form. Theoretically, form follows function, but once members have found a form that works, they cling to it.

4. Leadership in HPSs is strong and clear. It is not ambivalent. There is no question of the need for initiative or of its appropriate source (although this may not always be the same person). Leadership style varies widely from HPS to HPS, but it is remarkably consistent within a given HPS. Leadership style is never conflicted: it does not swing between cool and warm, close and distant, or demanding and laissez-faire. Leaders are reliable and predictable.

5. HPSs are fertile sources of inventions and new methods within the scope of the task they have defined and within the form they have chosen. HPSs are relatively conservative about new methods and inventions that take them outside the task boundaries

and structural forms they have traditionally practiced: they "do not tamper with a good thing."

6. HPSs are clearly bounded from their environments, and a considerable amount of energy, particularly on the part of leaders, is usually devoted to maintaining these boundaries. Bounding occurs in terms of firm, even if unofficial, membership rules, methods (technologies) employed, times and time durations in which the system is on, and the spaces the system occupies when it is operating. There is a strong consciousness that "we are different." These ongoing bounding efforts are among the ways in which this consciousness displays itself most clearly.

7. Proposition 6 leads to another consistent finding—that HPSs are often seen as a problem by entities in their environment, even those entities that have a great deal of power over them. HPSs avoid external control. They scrounge resources from the environment nonapologetically. They produce what they want by their standards, not what someone else wants. Thus they often frustrate environmental entities, especially in bureaucratic settings. One can note continual annoyance, even fury, with HPSs. People decide, "They've got to be broken up." This is especially true when an HPS is a subunit of a larger organization. The HPS is thus a paradox: it fulfills the larger system's desire for high performance, but the price is a relatively unmanageable subunit.

8. Above all, HPSs are systems that have "jelled," even though the phenomenon is very difficult to talk about. Neither mechanical nor organic metaphors are usually adequate for describing the "fit" of the system's various elements and practices. Frequently the elements of an HPS, when examined one at a time, do not seem to qualify for membership; HPSs are often composed of castoffs and rejects.

Beyond its concrete existence, the phenomenon of the HPS poses social science with a profound conceptual challenge—namely, that of learning to talk about intense human interdependency in terms more descriptively accurate than those provided by either physics or biology.

These propositions are what used to be called "clinical uniformities," which were made on the basis of intensive study of individual cases. The propositions can be illustrated and certainly debated, but they are difficult to prove unequivocally. Each of these propositions, furthermore, could be discussed at much greater length. Each contains many unitary observations of, to me, great fascination. In the rest of this chapter, however, I am going to restrict myself to the implications of propositions 1 and 4.

The Role of Clarity of Purposes

Many writers on large-system leadership have stressed the importance of purposes. A fundamental remark is this one by Chester Barnard: "An objective purpose that can serve as the basis for a cooperative system is one that is *believed* by the contributors (or potential contributors) to it to be the determined purpose of the organization. The *inculcation of belief* in the real existence of a common purpose is an essential executive function" (Emphasis added; Barnard, 1938, p. 87).

This observation captures, albeit awkwardly, the problematic character of purposes. They are not given; they do not exist independent of members' perceptions and values or of the "pictures in their heads," as I called purposes above. Yet the implication of Barnard's remark is that the relativity of purposes—that they *do* depend on perceptions—is not something that should be prominent in members' minds as they go about the organization's work. "Why are we doing this? Why are we doing it this way?" are questions we would prefer not to have people asking whenever they feel like it. Can an organization act and at the same time be questioning the grounds of its action—doubting, as it were? Such a dual awareness is an attractive notion to those who philosophize about the consciousness of the truly civilized person, but one may question the idea's extension to the collective level. Systemic doubt is quite another matter.

The political scientist Norton Long put the matter of the leader's role with respect to doubts and second thoughts quite trenchantly some years ago in an extraordinary essay in which he said:

> In the everyday routine of life, the problematic nature of reality is made up of a multiplicity of potentially applicable norms cutting in different directions, a fragmentary state of information, an absence of any relevant substantial amount of scientific knowledge, and a pressure of time flooding by constraining decision on the most precarious definition of the situation. . . . The reduction of the political problem [that is, of effective action] to a scientific problem is a natural result of the confusion of propositions of value and propositions of fact. It is also a result of the human desire to escape the sheer anguish of creative decision. *Leadership is concerned with the transformation of doubts into the psychological grounds of cooperative common action* [emphasis added; Long, 1963, p. 126].

Twenty-five years ago, Philip Selznick, in his landmark book, *Leadership in Administration*, proposed the "definition of institutional mission and role" and the "institutional embodiment of purpose" as being two essential functions of his "institutional leader" (Selznick, 1957, chaps. 3 and 4). In these three sets of ideas, there is a quality of "ongoingness" that has often been overlooked. In my own experiences with management groups, I frequently encounter an impatience, even an exasperation, with discussions of basic purposes. It is as if leaders would rather believe either that these matters are understood once and for all by organization members, or that the ongoingness occurs by a kind of osmosis—but that, in any case, the leaders have no responsibility to creatively revivify purposes.

This impatience may be justified in a stable world. A pervasive sense of purpose in an organization endures, after all, in relation to other forces, and as long as these are stable and predictable, purposes will probably continue to mean what they have always meant. But, as we all know, these other forces are themselves in motion. Most important among these forces in my opinion are the following four categories:

1. *Environmental demands and opportunities*. The more heterogeneous and dynamic these are, the more they present the organization with an ongoing need to interpret and reinterpret what is going on. It can take nothing for granted. The changing equivocality of environmental signals must constantly be removed.

2. *Organization members' needs, expectations, abilities, and values*. These constitute the changing world brought into the organization. By the nature of the organization itself, they must literally be "incorporated," and in the process it is frequently necessary to renegotiate the meaning of the organization's purpose.

3. *The technologies the organization employs in pursuit of its purposes*. These entail learning time to exploit their productive and economic potential. If the organization is constantly "upgrading" its technologies, it may never reach a smooth flow of habituated actions, a flow on which the economics of efficiency and profitable action are based.

4. *The phenomenon of reorganization itself*. This is less often noted than the previous three. Many more structural alternatives exist for the modern large system than existed twenty-five years ago, and many organizations are continually experimenting with new forms. The impact of these changes on role relationships, chains of command, felt senses of accountability, and so forth is not as thoroughly discussed as it should be, particularly the impact of all this flux on purposes.

In other words, the extent to which members can come to share pictures in their heads about the organization's basic purposes depends on some degree of stability in (1) environmental demands, (2) members' own expectations and needs, (3) the technologies they are operating, and (4) the structures through which they are bound together. *Beyond some unknown threshold, too much change in this system of factors breaks down the shared sense of what the organization is, why it exists, and what its basic purposes are.*

This is the key implication of Emery and Trist's famous remark that in their Type IV–Turbulent Field, "the ground itself is moving" (Emery and Trist, 1965). The moving-ground metaphor refers to the more basic paradigms and images that we use to organize experience. It is one thing for the objectives and techniques that flow from a paradigm to be rapidly changing, but when the paradigm itself is undergoing substantial revision, there is no longer a firm basis for any proposal.

Emery and Trist were aware of the leadership problems this situation creates, but they did not deal with the question at any length. They suggested that Douglas McGregor's Theory Y seemed to hold promise, which was a plausible expectation in the early 1960s but is, I think, considered to be quite insufficient today. They speculated prophetically about the ability of matrix structures to absorb large amounts of ambiguity. They were convinced that the articulation of overarching values is a crucial step. They seemed to be saying that even if *things* cannot be stabilized, consciousness might be, through the development of broadly shared values. *Paradigm* leadership was needed; that was the apparent thrust of their argument.

Others, of course, were issuing similar calls in the 1960s when the first pains of the collapsing paradigm were felt. ("This is the Age When Things Have Not Turned Out as We Thought They Would," said David Matthews on being sworn in as secretary of Health, Education, and Welfare in the early 1970s.) But even now, a decade later, I think the question of leadership under conditions of extreme turbulence is no nearer to a working solution than it was when first articulated twenty or thirty years ago. With the current Republican administration determined to increase freedom of action in the private sector, the question may be even more acute. If the need is for paradigm leadership and through national policy we undertake to give decision makers more freedom to act, it remains a kind of grand wager that these leaders will respond with forward-looking purposes for the 1990s and beyond.

So we must ask, more urgently than ever, what becomes of the "inculcation of belief" (Barnard), the "embodiment of purpose" (Selznick), and the "transformation of doubts" (Long)? What does this behavior look like in the first place? Under increasingly turbulent conditions, how does it change? Who among the leaders of the world's organizations, of whatever kind, is doing this work well?

First of all, the behavior we are talking about needs a name. I propose the word *purposing* to refer to *that continuous stream of actions by an organization's formal leadership that has the effect of inducing clarity, consensus, and commitment regarding the organization's basic purposes*. I decided on the term *purposing* as a result of investigating the etymology of the word *purpose* and discovering that it and the word *propose* derive from the same Latin root, *proponere*. In other words, through the filters of Old and Middle French and English our thinking has come to divide an idea that was originally more unified: that there is *both* an ongoing stream of proposings and the results of the process—purposes. We need the new word, *purposing*, to remind ourselves that a special class of proposings needs to occur in organizations—proposings that have to do with the establishment, clarification, and modification of purposes. This, I propose, we call purposing.

The Functions of Purposing

With the idea of purposing in hand, it is possible to begin to indicate some of the forms it takes in organizations. In general, my argument is that HPSs are, among other things, systems in which we can observe the phenomenon of purposing working well. People are not mixed up about why the system exists or about what their role in it is. Of course leaders do not refer to what they do as purposing; nevertheless, they inculcate belief, transform doubts, and embody purpose.

From HPSs as well as from other settings, I have identified the following seven functions of purposing:

1. *Purposing occurs in relation to the expectations of those who own or charter the system.* This does not mean that leaders merely preach conformity to these expectations but rather that the content of what they talk about and do is seen to have these key outside forces as reference points.

2. *Purposing is seen in the articulation of the grounds for basic strategic decisions.* These decisions may be of many different kinds: to add a particular person to the system, to change its posture toward systems with which it competes, to adopt new technology, to fundamentally alter its internal structure, and so forth. The point is that such decisions are not made or explained in isolation from basic purposes.

3. *Purposing is seen in leaders' accounts of the meaning of the system's daily activity.* The hours people put in, the skills they practice to acquire, the sacrifices they make, the pains they take, and the pains they experience—all these can be interpreted in terms of the system's basic purposes, and in HPSs it is a very noticeable phenomenon.

4. *Purposing is evident in decisions NOT to do things.* Examples include the decision not to offer proposed new products, enter new territories, add available new technology, or hire or retain particular people. The phrases "It's not us," "It wouldn't be right for us," and so forth are frequently heard in HPSs, as Thomas J. Peters mentioned in his study of America's best-managed companies (Peters and Waterman, 1982). Attractive-options-forgone is one of the most powerful forms of purposing. It communicates and inculcates discipline.

5. *Purposing differentiates the organization from other superficially similar organizations.* Members of every organization are conscious of what other systems somewhat like their own are doing. A key process by which they come to identify with their own organization is being helped to see how it is not quite like any other—how their own organization has a unique identity. This process of identification is a phenomenon that needs to be much more widely understood.

6. *Purposing is the expression of what the leadership wants.* In the social science literature, preoccupation with what the boss wants is often treated as a kind of neurotic dependency reaction. But it is possible to be curious and concerned in a healthy way about what the boss wants.

It is important to distinguish here between wanting something for the system and wanting something for oneself. The leadership of many large systems today is "just passing through," "getting a ticket punched," "on a fast track." Self-aggrandizement and self-promotion are often these leaders' basic motives. The worst thing in the world, some of them seem to feel, is actually to become entangled in the system.

I have never found an HPS whose leadership was perceived by members as on a fast track to something else. To be perceived as wanting something for the system is crucial. And it cannot be faked.

7. *Purposing in some sense entails the mythologizing of oneself and the organization.* When Selznick speaks of the institutional embodiment of purpose, one aspect of the process is to let oneself come to embody the organization. Perhaps people find it easier to identify with a person than with a complex social system. This means that the leadership becomes a kind of vessel or vehicle. In the way leaders talk and act, in the preferences they express, in their passions and tantrums, meanings echo for members. Harrison Owen, a longtime observer of large-system machinations in Washington, D.C., speaks of the leader needing to become the center of a "myth-modification process"—as an articulator of the new "likely stories," as Owen calls them, that can become the basis for future action.

To be willing to become a mythic figure is perhaps the true expression of the "loneliness of command." The loneliness derives from the felt discrepancy between what one is feeling and how one knows a contemplated action will be received by members and the organization's public. The search, agonizing as it may be, is for courses of action that are responsive to the ownership (function 1), substantively sound (function 2), not merely demagogic or exploitative (function 3), consistent with the system's evolving identity (functions 4 and 5), and honest expressions of one's own values (function 6).

No wonder it is so difficult; no wonder it is rare—although it is not as rare as some might think.

In HPSs, men and women are finding ways to conduct purposing in terms of the characteristics I have just discussed. This is why HPSs are such powerful and instructive exemplars. The final section of this chapter is concerned with synthesizing many of these remarks into a simple statement of what leaders of HPSs actually do.

The Purposing of High-Performing Systems

I believe that three characteristics appear 100 percent of the time in the actions of leaders of HPSs. I think these three characteristics and their interrelationships have profound implications for the world of organizations and organizational leaders, not because they are such esoteric or mysterious factors, but because they are so well known that they are apparently easily overlooked.

1. Leaders of HPSs put in extraordinary amounts of *time*.
2. Leaders of HPSs have very strong *feelings* about the attainment of the system's purposes.
3. Leaders of HPSs *focus* on key issues and variables.

I have come to call this the *time-feeling-focus theory* of HPS leadership. There are, of course, many nuances, subtleties, and local specialties connected with the leadership of any HPS, but over and over again, time, feeling, and focus appear no matter what else appears. They may not be totally sufficient in themselves, but they are necessary to the leadership of HPSs. In this section, I say a few more words about each, following which I will describe what happens in human systems when one or two of the three are absent. I then conclude with some comments about the interrelationships of leader and system development, and about the question of leadership style.

Time

Leaders of HPSs work very hard. This is basic. They put in many hours. Their consciousness is dominated by the system's issues and events. They often see the rest of life in terms of the system's jargon, technology, and culture. Their awareness of the system does not respect the clock, and hence they can be seen scribbling notes to themselves or others, making phone calls, and replaying and debriefing system events at all kinds of odd times—evenings, weekends, vacation periods, the wee hours. Their consciousness does not respect place either: they work in the office, at home, in airport boarding areas, in the back seats of taxicabs, or anywhere else they happen to be. At halftimes and intermissions, they duck out to call the office. They are often perceived by system members and others as living, eating, sleeping, breathing the system.

The hours they put in are matters of frequent comment by those around them. Stories accumulate about the amounts of time they put in and about their nonstop work habits. Curiously, the quality of what they accomplish in all these hours is commented on much less frequently—not because the quality is thought to be mediocre or low, but because it is apparently felt to be a natural result of all those many hours of extraordinary effort.

It is of great importance that these leaders put in large amounts of both microtime and macrotime. Microtime is the hour-to-hour, day-to-day kind of investment. Less frequently noted is macrotime: leaders of HPSs tend to stay in their jobs for many years; they do not simply "pass through." They make a large commitment of both microtime and macrotime.

Sometimes the HPS is a rather temporary system—that is, it is not intended to last indefinitely. In such a case, macrotime is the willingness to "commit for the duration."

Feeling

Leaders of HPSs care deeply about the system. This includes its purposes, its structure and conduct, its history, and its future security, and although this is sometimes expressed in a way that would make a psychologist shudder, they care about the people in the system. For the leader of an HPS, constant energetic purposing is a natural expression of feeling—that is, of his or her own deep values and beliefs. Purposing is not a style or function that is adopted for some occasion. Feeling furthermore sustains the person through many hours of labor, discussed in the section on time. Involvement with the system is the person's life, which is why, from his or her frame of reference, the amount of time put in is a natural thing to do.

Macrotime often plays a key role in the development and expression of feeling. With many large systems, it is not immediately clear what makes them special. A leader "cycling through" on an eighteen- to twenty-four-month assignment may never experience the system much more deeply than its immediate issues permit. Many, many executives bring high achievement motivation to their jobs. In macrotime this motivation becomes invested in the system's culture and this culture comes to be seen as something valuable for its own sake rather than as a vehicle for the leader's ambition, development, and next assignment.

Motivation in HPSs, I said, has "peculiarity." In leaders this peculiarity can be seen in the way they have integrated their innate energies and ambitions with the system's needs and opportunities.

Selznick's "institutional embodiment of purpose," therefore, is not a one-way phenomenon. In HPSs there is a two-way embodiment in feeling of leader-in-system and system-in-leader. When a person becomes "Mr . . . [whatever the activity or industry is]" or "the First Lady of . . . [the activity or industry]," the two-way embodiment is complete.

Through feeling, leaders of HPSs tend to take themselves and their systems quite seriously. They often become the targets of worldly-wise cynics and satirists. For example, such leaders' total absorption makes them vulnerable to interpretations of their behavior that are askance from the values and beliefs they hold. Some years ago in the *Harvard Business Review*, Seymour Tilles compared the strategy used by the founder of Lestoil to beat Procter & Gamble with Hadrian's strategy. *The New Yorker* quoted a key paragraph from that article in one of its famous column footings with the editorial remark, "Every age has its heroes."

More seriously, the very strength of feeling can sometimes blind leaders to what the system needs as the environment changes. They sometimes cannot see that the meanings they have built up about the system may be becoming maladaptive, that they have to rethink what the system is and what it can be in the new conditions. All organizations go through this process and HPSs are not immune. Their conservatism about new methods and the boundaries that separate them from the environment are in continuous tension with the dynamic environment. When a system drifts into mediocrity over time, it is usually the result of a combination of very strong feeling on the part of leaders and members and insufficient wisdom about the next element discussed—focus.

Focus

Management literature frequently discusses what the boss ought to be working on. Chester Barnard's original essay (1938) was devoted to this question. Situational leadership theory has been answering this question in recent years with "The boss ought to be working on whatever the system needs at the moment." Leaders of HPSs have solved this problem. Behind attention to detail, which is possible because of time, one can note persistent factors that they focus on. In one system attention may be focused on recruitment, in another on the securing of stable funding, in another on the buffering of the system from the environment, and in another on hands-on involvement in the system's basic activity. There seems to be no fixed formula, no short list of variables that are always important. But I believe that there always is some short list of priorities that leaders have clearly in mind—that is, in focus.

Furthermore, one can note leaders actively communicating their judgments about what is important to members. They help bring focus to others' behavior as well as their own. This function is of extreme importance because in any organization, at any moment, there are many things that need attention. These factors do not exist as abstract impersonal matters but rather are actively voiced by various organization members. The organization is a texture of proposings, as I said earlier. Leaders of HPSs are not distracted by this cacophony. They know which few things are important, and in their statements and actions they make these priorities known. Members also learn what is important in macrotime, and, therefore, in HPSs the cacophony of proposings is less chaotic and centrifugal than in other systems—although it is rarely absent entirely. Focus is really focusing in dynamic terms: it is an ongoing process of choosing what to emphasize and what to leave alone.

Strategic planning and strategic management, as they are discussed in the literature, are primarily the study of focus. What are the key variables? In Thomas J. Peters's survey of America's best-managed companies (Peters and Waterman, 1982), excellent companies are found to have "simultaneous loose-tight controls"—that is, they have picked out key variables and developed tight controls over them and are willing to use relatively loose controls over the rest. Such an approach at one and the same time communicates what is important and a desire to allow as much freedom and latitude as possible.

Without time and feeling, strategic planning, as discussed in the bulk of the current literature, is an empty technical exercise. For example, one of the most common problems in strategic management is the length of view that top managers take. It tends to be too short. Their term of office does not extend far enough into the future. They will not be around when the fruits (or poisons) of their decisions appear. This is why the concept of macrotime is so important. Focus constitutes the *what* of executive leadership, but it cannot carry by itself the *why* or the *when* or the *how*. The *why* resides primarily in feeling, the *when*, in time. The *how*, as I will show, is not as important—in HPSs at least—as writers on leadership have made it.

Variations on Time-Feeling-Focus

I have said that these three elements are always present in the actions of leaders of HPSs. It is instructive to pause and comment on situations in which one or two or all three are absent. Some very familiar patterns emerge.

1. *Time with no feeling or focus*. The phenomena associated with workaholism and Type A behavior are inherent in this situation and the next. The investment of large chunks of time without a positive feeling that the activity is important and without a focus on key issues has the quality of compulsiveness. There are extreme forms that are, indeed, neurotic, because with this pattern we are talking about a person who works very hard without knowing exactly what to work on or why. Attention to detail and the investment of time alone is not characteristic of HPS leaders.

2. *Time and feeling without focus*. The leader who cares deeply and is willing to work very hard, but for whom everything seems to

be of equal importance, is a somewhat tragic figure. In large and complex organizations this mix of factors can be an actual killer. Managers who speak of having to run harder and harder just to stay in the same place may be stuck in this pattern. The person who has time and feeling without focus needs help in understanding the system and in managing her or his own time. It is to this person that we say, "You need to step back and really think about what is important." Sadly, though, the person caught in the grip of this mix misinterprets the advice. He or she thinks the advice is "Put in less time; don't feel so strongly." Of course, the person can't do it and doesn't even want to do it. Time and feeling are deep expressions of the person's history and character and are not easily modified. How such a person learns to focus without cutting back on time or feeling is a major challenge to students of executive development.

3. *Time and focus without feeling.* This is, I am afraid, characteristic of a large number of the young people we see today in our professional schools of management. I quickly add that the cultures of the schools themselves tend to reward this pattern lavishly, so even a young person not initially disposed toward this pattern will feel enormous pressure to adopt it.

Time and focus without feeling says, "Don't get too involved. Look at the facts. Make a decision and move on to the next thing. Be willing to work hard because there is no free lunch, but don't get your identity too wrapped up in what you are doing. Build your track record, get your tickets punched, do quality work at each milestone on the fast track. Somewhere out in your future—in your forties, perhaps—you'll have accumulated the 'clout' to do what you want to do and be the person you want to be. You'll have earned the right to feeling." Unfortunately, for too many, the forties do not bring this opportunity; instead they bring a set of work habits and personal financial circumstances that seem to require continuation of the same patterns.

It is important to say that with time and focus without feeling, the pattern is not dysfunctional per se. It is just never found in leaders of HPSs. Some occupations, for example, require that feeling be detached from the immediate system in favor of adherence to standards and procedures that are independent of the system—that is, they derive from another system of which the person is a member. There is no question that this displacement of feeling from an immediate system to some broader professional system is socially important. Law, medicine, and accounting are examples. The possibility of a "high-performing relationship" with an immediate client is sometimes a secondary consideration compared with adhering to professional standards.

4. *Feeling without time or focus.* This condition is usually labeled as idealism or cynicism. It is possible to care very deeply about various organizations in society without actually devoting much time to them or really understanding what is involved in operating them effectively (focus). Without the commitment of energy expressed in time and the thought and practicality expressed in focus, the feeling-driven person issues calls to arms or fulminates. Again, this is a social role that is historically of great importance, but it is not found in HPS leaders.

5. *Feeling and focus without time.* Three very well-known social roles frequently manifest this pattern. The staff person who does very good work but who goes home at five o'clock is one example. The astute social commentator is a second. The person engaged in one of America's fastest-growing industries—consulting—is the third. A good consultant focuses his or her efforts on the right variables and cares that the client organization does better. But consultants are not continuously present. They phase in and out. They often are not there when the system needs them most. Their function is not to sustain the system but to get it started, to get it pointed in the right direction. So once again, it is not that having feeling and focus without time is bad or dysfunctional per se, but rather that this mix is not found in HPS leaders.

6. *Focus without time or feeling.* This describes a person who is working on the right things but who is not putting in more hours

than absolutely necessary and for whom there is no very deep personal meaning in the activity. This mix is never found in HPS leadership. Actually, this pattern describes an "employee," whose focus comes from someone else who has defined the task carefully. Such a person just works the expected hours at the expected energy level. Focus without time or feeling is just a job.

7. *Absence of time, feeling, and focus.* So far I have described situations in which one or two of the three elements are strongly present. What about the situations in which none of them is present to any significant degree? I am not concerned with diagnosing pervasive organizational or societal ills in this chapter. My HPS research, however, causes me to constantly wonder: to what extent have we drifted into a broad social condition where one can be a member or even a leader of an organization without time or feeling or focus as I have defined them? It is a sobering exercise to reflect on all the social forces today that work against the investment of time, the flowering of feeling, and the attainment of focus.

Relation of Time, Feeling, and Focus to System Development

The three factors seem to be interrelated and interdependent, although they do not exist in direct causal relationships one to another. In retrospect, however, we can see in the actions and attitudes of HPS leaders how investments of time tend to deepen feeling, how the development of feeling leads to putting in more time, how focus both is expressive *of* time and feeling and leads *to* further investments of time and new patterns of feeling. I emphasize that these relationships are noticed in retrospect. One cannot say, prospectively, that putting in time, for example, will automatically deepen feeling and make more likely the discovery of the key variables captured in the idea of focus.

That strength in one factor does not automatically cause development in the other two suggests that some additional forces are present in the development of HPS leaders that are relatively absent in the development of leaders of other systems. Such forces lie in the system itself; the system's developing strength and success somehow make more likely the discovery of the key things to focus on, the willingness to put in time, and the development of ever-stronger feeling about the system and its purposes.

There is a good deal of anecdotal evidence to support this idea. For example, most of us, at one time or another, have experienced success in some organizational effort that seemed to trigger a collection of improvements in the system in a sometimes startling fashion. Effort got more efficient, morale jumped, members' confidence in each other increased apace, and leadership improved in a variety of ways, including the three factors I have been discussing. Sometimes such systems get on a "streak" where, for a period at least, they just seem to do everything right. A process like this, I am suggesting, little understood as it is, could be quite a significant influence on the development of the system's leadership. We know, of course, that "nothing succeeds like success."

A second kind of evidence that suggests that the evolving success of the system has a powerful developmental effect on the leadership comes from the way members of HPSs talk about the early formative period of the system. Consistently they come out with such statements as "We had no idea things would turn out like this," "In the early years, we hardly knew what we were doing," "We were really groping," or "We just did what we thought we were supposed to do." I have never found an HPS member who claimed that the high achievements of the system were merely the logical results of a preexisting plan, although the notion of "having a dream and seeking to realize it" is very common. Nor do I have data from members or leaders of HPSs that suggest that the leaders knew all along what they were doing. In an HPS, omniscient strategies are usually not attributed to the leadership.

So, in summary, my current thinking is that the grasp of time, feeling, and focus by the leader develops and coexists with the sys-

tem's life and achievements. This, however, is not a particularly satisfying way to talk about leadership in HPSs. More tempting is the
assertion that "leaders cause high-performing systems." That certainly is the thrust of much of the writing on management and leadership—that if the individual somehow does something to his or
her attitude, knowledge, or style, major system improvements will
occur. Social scientists have implicitly been promising this to practitioners for years. Marginal improvements do seem to occur in some
cases, but I have no evidence that the breakthrough to a high-
performing condition as I have defined it will occur.

I said earlier that HPSs have "jelled" in a way that cannot be
easily discussed in our current language system of mechanical and
organic metaphors. That finding is relevant to this question of the
relationship between the leader's attitude and behavior and the
development of the system. One reason I think the time-feeling-
focus model has promise is that it is simple. It does not overcatego-
rize and overspecify what it is we are trying to understand. Similarly,
the eight broad generalizations about HPSs given at the beginning
of this chapter are deliberately phrased in as commonsense a way as
possible. I am trying to keep our attention on the experience of
members and leaders in these settings.

I have discussed the time-feeling-focus approach to this point as
a way of understanding leaders' behavior. The scheme is also very
useful for understanding members' behavior and for understanding
the system as a whole. With due regard for the different roles they
play and scopes of responsibility they carry, time-feeling-focus can
be used to evaluate anyone in the HPS.

It is not just the leader but the system as a whole that can be
seen functioning at all sorts of odd times and in odd places. Members come in on evenings and weekends. The culture of the system
blends into the cultures of their families. These are manifestations
of the time factor. Congruence of feeling, as I have said several
times, is a distinguishing characteristic of an HPS. What I called
the peculiarity of motivation is shared and intensely valued among

members. Focus as an intermember phenomenon is one of the most striking features of an HPS as contrasted with other human systems. In an HPS, people actually agree, without having to go through tortuous processes of negotiation and conflict management, on what the key factors are.

Perhaps an HPS is not an objective entity at all. The criteria by which its success is measured are subjective. The meanings it transmits to members and observers in its environment are intensely personal and subjective. It is full of all kinds of events and processes that social science has tended to ignore. Statements like these, of course, could be made about all social systems. They are all objects of consciousness in the first instance and as such should not be reduced to simple machine models, cause-effect models, or other superficially attractive metaphors. I think phenomenology has the most interesting things to say about these issues, but an exploration of these things is beyond the scope of this chapter. Suffice it to say, for the moment, that I regard an HPS as a frame on which members' consciousnesses interact. The interesting thing about leaders' consciousness is that it seems to be described by the time-feeling-focus scheme.

The Question of Style

The time-feeling-focus idea leads to the final observation that a leader's style does not seem to determine the level of the system's performance. Therefore, what I've learned about HPSs seems to differ radically from the views that have been expressed in the management literature over the last twenty-five years—that is, that managerial and leadership style has a definite effect on the organization's performance. Perhaps the problem lies in the fact that most research in this area has been carried out in low-performing systems. Thus researchers have frequently concluded that the *way* the leader or manager was working—his or her style—was having a significantly negative effect on performance. They have extrapolated from this conclusion to the idea that a change in style will repair the damage that is being done to motivation, morale, communication, trust, and problem solving. I need not review further the thousands of pages on the subject of warm versus cool, participative versus autocratic, and demanding versus accepting styles. My main point is that, for the most part, all this interest in style is beside the point *in high-performing systems*.

I have seen every style I can conceive of in the leadership of HPSs. There are tyrants whose almost maniacal commitment to achieving the system's purposes makes one think that they'd be locked up if they were not in charge of an organization that was the best of its kind. There are warm, laid-back parental figures who hardly seem to be doing anything at all, until one looks a little more closely. There are technocrats devoted to computerized representations of the system, and dreamers who seem to care nothing about the operational data. Some of these leaders are educated to the highest levels, and others never finished high school. Owing to the focus factor, they all possess expertise in what the system does, but some express this expertise constantly, and others don't. Some seem clearly to be Type A's on the way to exhaustion or an early grave, but most are in good health and of noticeably strong constitution. Some are rah-rah optimists and others are dour critics who express their love for the system by enumerating its imperfections. Leaders of HPSs are all over the style map.

What the theory described in this chapter says to the would-be leader is "Seek constantly to do what is right and what is needed in the system (focus). Do it continually in terms of your energy (time). Put your whole psyche into it (feeling)." This is the normative lesson I derive from studying HPS leaders. It is a very simple prescription, and in its simplicity it is somewhat at variance with the fine and precise distinctions in the literature. But my results suggest that the fundamental role of these three factors is that they are always understood in combination rather than one at a time.

Conclusion

In HPSs, as I have defined them, one can note constant purposing by the system leadership. Purposing occurs through the investment of large amounts of micro-and macrotime, the experience and expression of very strong feeling about the attainment of purposes and the importance of the system, and the attainment of understanding of the key variables for system success (focus). All leaders of HPSs have integrated these three factors at a very high level of intensity and clarity.

The number of social scientists who are trying to understand excellence in human systems is very small. Pathology is more accessible and, for some, more fun. The question of what it takes to govern and lead an HPS and the question of how we are going to develop more men and women who are equipped to do so await the increased attention that I believe HPSs deserve. This chapter has been an effort to stimulate such attention.

4

Visionary Leadership

To begin our consideration of leadership and vision and their role in organizations, consider the following quotation. The question is, what sort of an organization would describe itself this way?

Messenger of sympathy and love
Servant of parted friends
Consoler of the lonely
Bond of the scattered family
Enlarger of the common life
Carrier of news and knowledge
Instrument of trade and industry
Promoter of mutual acquaintance
Of peace and of goodwill
Among men and nations.

There are probably several kinds of organizations that might describe themselves this way. In fact, these ten lines are literally chiseled in stone across the facade of the main building of the U.S. Postal Service in downtown Washington, D.C. The building dates

Note: This chapter was originally published as Chapter Two in A. R. Cohen (ed.), *The Portable MBA in Management*. New York: Wiley, 1993, pp. 12–37. Reprinted in slightly edited form with permission of John Wiley & Sons, Inc.

from 1912, that is, from a time when the Postal Service was the Post *Office*; from a time when United Parcel Service, Federal Express, and other private sector competitors did not exist; from a time when a first-class letter cost a nickel to send and "special delivery" meant your package would get to its destination by the next day; from a time when "neither snow, nor rain, nor heat, nor gloom of night stays these couriers from the swift completion of their appointed rounds."

The fact that today's Postal Service may be having more difficulty fulfilling the vision embodied in the ten-line inscription than it once did does not detract from the importance of the subject of the role that vision plays in organizational life. In fact, that a vision can be "overtaken by events" is what has made the subject important! If visions could be articulated once and for all with no fear of becoming obsolete or irrelevant, the issue would not occupy the place it has come to occupy in management education over the past twenty years. This whole question of the durability of vision will receive extensive treatment later in this chapter.

For the moment, though, let us consider the inscription for its own sake. It captures an essential quality of *vision* as it will be discussed in this chapter. We define *vision* as an expression that does not merely describe why an organization exists and what products and services it intends to deliver. A vision is a portrayal of an organization's intended activities and character in vivid terms that capture the organization's human meaning and value. A vision is full of possibility. A vision is a motivational statement as much as it is a descriptive statement. It expresses the *feeling* that those who hold it have for the organization and its work. We will call the bare statement of why the organization exists and what it intends to do the mission. We will call its human meaning and the difference that the mission makes in the world the vision. If the mission is the words, the vision is the music.

This chapter treats the process of creating and effectively communicating vision as the essential characteristic of leadership. There are many things a leader must know and be able to do. I will argue that a vision of what the organization and its products and services mean to its customers, its employees, and its other key constituents needs to be interwoven in leadership. Put another way, leadership behavior that is not infused with vision is not truly leadership.

This chapter is organized in four broad sections. We first consider at greater length what role the vision plays in the organization. The guiding question is, what is vision and what does it do? Included in this section is a discussion of why the whole subject has recently become much more important in management education and management practice. The second section then discusses the creation of visions by leaders. What are they doing when they are "envisioning"? In particular, I elaborate on the statement I made that for organizational behavior to be *leadership* it must have vision woven all through it. The third section discusses in some detail various methods for making vision real for organization members. In many ways, it is the most important section of the chapter and covers one of the most important problems in management practice today. After a leader has created a vision, how does he or she make it meaningful to others in the organization and among its external constituents? In the final section I discuss certain special problems of vision in organizations—problems that are occasioned by other trends and events in organizations and in the wider world. A key premise of this section is that even as the subject of vision has become more and more important, it is also becoming more and more difficult. The chapter ends, therefore, with a somewhat paradoxical view of a world of organizations in greater need than ever before of men and women who can bring vision to their work as leaders.

Before proceeding with these topics, though, I would like to explain the tone of this chapter. I assume that you are interested in leadership and vision because you would like to be a person who leads with vision, that is, that you have a personal vision of actively using the ideas in this chapter. I assume that it is not just curiosity that brings you to this chapter and book, but a desire to give living meaning to these ideas.

This concept of the reader or learner in an action role is in fact the hallmark of professional education, for management as well as for law, medicine, or engineering. Professional education, as distinct from purely academic education, assumes that the learner is actually going to do what is being discussed and will do it at a high level of quality and in keeping with the standards of the profession. Thus, the tone of this chapter is action-oriented, and I quite honestly intend to motivate as well as inform you.

What Is Vision and What Does It Do?

The nature of vision and the role it plays in human organizations is not as elusive or exotic as one might think from listening to all the rhetoric about the need for women and men of vision in our society. Vision is very common and ordinary; indeed, its power lies in its commonness and ordinariness. Vision's common and ordinary quality can be illustrated by a simple exercise in reflection.

I invite you to think about the best experience you have ever had in an organization—the most memorable experience, one that you look back on fondly, that you enjoy thinking and talking about, even bragging about. It doesn't matter what kind of an organization it was or is, how important its mission was or is, or how famous or successful it was or is by the world's standards. Some to whom I ask this question are presently in the best situation they've ever been in, but many are not. Some hark back to college, their adolescence, or even childhood. Some mention their family, but most do not. For some it is a sports experience; others mention military experiences. Voluntary organizations such as fund-raising groups, political campaigns, or charities often get mentioned, as do performing arts troupes. The main thing is that you be able to say that this was the most meaningful or one of the most meaningful organizational experiences you have ever had. Take a moment before continuing and

think as fully as you can of what was or is for you "the best organizational experience I've ever had."

I have asked this question of hundreds of people. Rather uni-
formly, nearly everyone has had some experience that fits the above
evocation. Some people have many experiences to choose from;
others have relatively few. A huge range of experiences is reported.
Virtually every kind of organization imaginable gets mentioned by
one person or another. Typically, people are in some kind of membership role in the organization they are thinking of—an employee,
a dues-paying member, a volunteer. Occasionally people mention
being a customer of the organization they are thinking of, some
remember classes in which they were students, and others recall
hospitals in which they were patients. Interestingly, though, such
individuals *talk* like actual members of the organization, even
though technically they were not. Sometimes people remember
with awe not the organizations that they were members of but
rather organizations they *competed against*.

It is not uncommon for people to remember organizational experiences in which they had a primary leadership role, but seemingly
just as many people remember experiences in which they were in a
relatively lowly position.

The thing that is most striking about all these experiences,
despite their concrete variety, is what prompts the writing of this
chapter: in one way or another, all of these memories are infused
with a *vision* of what the organization was, of what it was trying to
do, of what it could be, of what it meant to the people involved with
it. Ask people to recall the best organizational experience they've
ever had and they don't just remember a "job," an "assignment," or
something they did for a while because they needed the money or
because it was a stepping-stone to something else. They remember
the fullness of the impact of the organization on them. They remember how it filled up their lives—how they lived, ate, slept, breathed
it. They remember, not always fondly, how hard they worked on
its behalf and the price they often paid to be involved with the

organization. They shake their head in wonderment even many years later that the organization could have had that strong an impact on them. Often there are tears and occasionally anger and regret. *Always* there are stories—stories that have to be told. Stories that are full of drama, humor, conflict, incredible demonstrations of talent and skill—of victory, of course, but of tragedy and defeat as well. I have inadvertently discovered that the reason soldiers tell war stories is that for many of them their experiences in battle are the most memorable things that have ever happened to them.

Stories are concrete, and concreteness is the hallmark of a vision that has taken hold deeply in the members' minds and feelings. Such a vision may start out merely as an idea or verbal statement, but if you're talking about the best experience you ever had, the vision will have moved beyond a mere idea for you and will have truly become the *spirit* of the organization. It is this spirit that is remembered so positively and vividly. And indeed, it is often remembered wonderingly: "It's amazing when you think about it," someone will say, thinking back, "how we could ever have gotten so wrapped up in the work and in each other. There's no way to explain it." "No way to explain it" embodies both the promise and the paradox of organizational visions. They exert an incredibly powerful tug on people's emotions and on their willingness to contribute, but exactly *how* this happens and whether it can deliberately be *made* to happen are quite different matters.

The point of this exercise has been to give you some sense of the role, the power, and the elusiveness of what we are calling vision. The principal thrust of this chapter is the challenge to leadership posed by this essential but rather mysterious phenomenon of organizational vision. For the moment, however, let me develop one more major theme that is present in the memories you have of your best organizational experiences.

One of the main reasons that the experience was so memorable for you is that there was some fit between the vision that existed in the organization and the personal needs, expectations, hopes, fears, and indeed visions of yourself that you brought to the situation. You may have had a hand in fashioning the vision that came alive, but your contribution was not geared purely to what was needed in the situation and to the organization's official mission. Your contribution also reflected what you wanted, were prepared to contribute, and were capable of: your potential and also your limits. The same can be said of everyone else who was in the situation with you.

The point is that organizational vision is not some independent thing, apart from the human beings in the situation. It partly reflects the official mission and the requirements of the situation, but it also reflects the personal aspirations and energies of those who are there. It draws its vividness and its force from people, not from "situations" or "problems." Vision is not a separate objective fact. It is instead a living expression of shared meaning and commitment. The power of vision lies not merely in its content and its appropriateness for the situation. The power lies with the content and appropriateness *combined* with the feeling among members of its being shared. No individual feels, "I'm the only one who is really committed to this project" in organizations for which the vision is truly working effectively. Instead, people feel, "I am part of something larger than myself—something I personally believe in, but something that everyone else really believes in, too." The vision is glue, binding people together in common effort and common values.

The phrase "a sense of common purpose" is often heard in connection with the "glue" that binds people together in common effort. For instructive purposes, this chapter treats the notions of a common vision and a common purpose as being very closely related and as different. Both phrases imply that a group shares a common positive meaning about something and that this meaning is energizing. The notion of vision stresses the clarity of *what* is felt to be meaningful—be it something tangible, like a building or a new product, or a desired event. The idea of purpose places more emphasis on the *desirability of pursuing* this thing, whatever it is. Purpose is the *reason* the thing is felt to be meaningful and desirable.

Leadership, as discussed in the next section, involves both of these two meanings: leaders both portray desirable states of affairs (visions) and give us reasons (purposes) for seeking the states of affairs. Vision and purpose combine to give organization members *clarity*, *consensus*, and *commitment*. (See Chapter Three.)

To return to the subject of our most memorable organizational experiences, there is another way to talk about all this—an approach that will connect this discussion to the challenges that organization leaders are facing today. In modern management parlance, you, the participant, are a "stakeholder" in the organization. The term is a brilliantly memorable extension of the meaning of the term *stockholder*. It was coined in the 1960s to capture the idea that more people and organizations than just those with an equity ownership stake (stockholders) care deeply about how an organization does. Even though these other stakeholders don't legally own the organization, they are not prevented from coming to have expectations of it and from trying to influence its direction. A word was needed to describe all those having a stake in the organization, because the 1960s saw an enormous expansion of the number of people and groups in society who began to assert their entitlement to influence society's institutions. The antiwar and civil rights movements were just two of the most visible and audible members of the rising chorus. Joining them were the women's movement, the free speech movement among students, various environmental protection groups, consumer advocacy groups, antismoking lobbies, gun control advocates, voter registration partisans, internationalists, advocates for the inner cities, white-collar unions, radical free-enterprisers, and me-generation self-developers—just to name a few of the more prominent new sets of stakeholders in society's major institutions.

This unprecedented explosion of would-be stakeholders created for all organizations an enormous dilemma: how to respond in good faith to the claims these groups were making without fragmenting in all directions the traditional visions of themselves that the organizations had been pursuing. I must emphasize that it was not just the business corporations that felt this upsurge of claims on visions of itself; it was any organization. No organizational leadership could afford to continue thinking of its organization in the way that it always had, once the exponential increase in the number and variety of stakeholders' demands really got under way. Some organizations were not able to adapt and either went out of existence or shrank into insignificance. But most major institutions were able to begin accommodating themselves—that is to say, refashioning their vision—to the social changes that were occurring. The ongoing accommodation continues to this day, for we have truly become a global "entitlement society" in which there is no way to predict who will define themselves as stakeholders and what claims, legitimate or not, they will assert.

The stakeholder idea can be applied to all organizations—public and private, profit and nonprofit, large and small, domestic and international. As just noted, there is virtually no limit to the number of those who might become stakeholders in a particular organization, but the most common groups are customers, suppliers, owners, regulators, neighbors, competitors, and—significantly— employees at all levels, including managers up to the top of the organization. Some organizations may have unique groups of stakeholders. For example, Johnson & Johnson, the giant pharmaceutical company, declares *babies* to be one of its most important groups of stakeholders (Rowe, Mason, and Dickel, 1986, p. 558). A nuclear power plant might have unborn generations as stakeholders, at least we would hope so, because of the long half-life of nuclear waste. Government agencies try to keep the "public interest" before them at all times, which is in effect a decision to define society at large as a stakeholder and to try not to let any single group of individuals (stakeholders) exercise undue influence. Government agencies, of course, do have continuing problems with special-interest groups who seek special treatment. All the more reason for such agencies to be as clear as they can be in their vision of the public interest!

One of the key things about the stakeholder idea is that the stakeholders define their own stake in the organization; the organization doesn't define it for them. As a stakeholder, you are working within your own set of expectations of what the organization should do for you. It is not an exaggeration to say that these expectations themselves are your vision—a vision of how the organization ought to work. It is what you were remembering about your best organizational experience: how the organization fulfilled your own vision. That's what made it a best experience *for you*. However, *all* the stakeholders are seeking the same thing, whether they are succeeding or not. The stake is the meaning that the stakeholder wants the organization to have, that is, what the consequences will be of a satisfactory or an unsatisfactory relationship.

The leadership and managerial stakeholders, as is now clear, are in a special position. Unlike everyone else, they have an official responsibility for the fulfillment of the organization's mission, the bare, unvarnished statement of why the organization exists and of what it intends to do. Leaders' and managers' principal stake is in the fulfillment of this mission. Their vision—their enrichment of the mission with energy and color—must be expressive of what the mission *means* to them. And their vision cannot ignore the visions of all the other stakeholders: all their expectations, needs, wishes, wants, aversions, prejudices, demands, and even threats.

Somehow, the vision of an organization's leadership must synthesize, integrate, and transform all the separate visions into an overarching one within which stakeholders can unite and cooperate effectively. The leadership's vision bears a constraint, in other words, that is true of no other stakeholder's: it must integrate as best it can all the other visions that are held. Even if the leadership is the first to articulate a vision, as in the case of a new business startup, it must still take account of the other visions the stakeholders will come to have.

The task is sobering—to confront all the various visions of the organization that are held by its various stakeholders and to realize that they do not necessarily have anything to do with each other! In other words, it is easy for an organization's leaders to find themselves juggling the conflicting expectations (visions) of its various stakeholders as to what proper conduct is. When Harlan Cleveland, one of the most insightful of modern commentators, calls modern organizational leadership the "get-it-all-together profession," he is speaking of just this juggling act (Cleveland, 1985, chap. 1). Organization leaders and managers frequently find themselves in an impossible cross fire, expected, as they say, to be all things to all people. It is not surprising that so many senior executives, especially profit-conscious business executives, resist new calls for social responsibility and increased service to their various stakeholders. It is not that they are irresponsible in some absolute sense, or that they necessarily deserve any of the other names they are frequently called, but rather that they are not eager to further complicate their lives with new stakeholders or higher levels of obligation to existing stakeholders. The job is already tough enough, in their view.

Thus, the stakeholder idea helps us to see the real leadership challenge that senior managers face. They are not free to ignore the idea of vision and make do with specific objectives, because then their objectives will simply be caught in the cross fire of other stakeholders' demands (visions). Nor are they free to arbitrarily declare their personal vision of what the organization should be and do, for they inevitably will come into conflict with other visions. They have no choice but to think of vision as something that must come to infuse the whole, with themselves as the principal inventors of how this can happen. They have to learn to incorporate the new perspectives into their views of the organization, no matter how clumsily and haltingly. This learning process is the number-one challenge facing organization leaders today. In the next section, we take up in more detail just what leadership with vision entails.

Leadership with Vision

It will be difficult to talk about visionary leadership if we are constantly pausing to note its dangers and defects. A great deal can go wrong with visionary leadership; it is not a panacea. But let us discuss how it works ideally in a leader's actions and how it works when a leader is acting competently and in good faith. It will be easier afterward to note some of the key assumptions and dangers.

"An executive ought to *want* something," said the late David S. Brown, long-time professor of public administration at George Washington University. Brown's remark is deceptively simple. Behind it are many years of observing executives in both the public and private sectors who don't seem to want anything in particular. They are content, apparently, to preside over the system pretty much as they find it. Their actions tend to be restricted to the problems that come *to* them. Of course, there is no dearth of such issues, so they can manage to stay very busy. However, to quote Russell Ackoff, one of the fathers of system theory and of strategic management, they are "reactive" leaders (Ackoff, 1974, p. 24). They are letting events—often crises—in the organization dictate their actions. They don't act until they have to. They are following a recipe without having exercised any choice over what dish they are cooking.

As noted in the preceding section, the pace of change in the late twentieth century has rendered the reactive style obsolete. It is forcing all organizations to decide anew what dishes they want to cook. The recipes from their past are only partially useful at best, and sometimes former recipes (strategies) will take them in directions where they absolutely should not want to go. To put this point explicitly in managerial terms, David Hurst, a Canadian steel executive and management writer, has said, "The present challenge to management is to innovate—to find tomorrow's business" (Hurst, 1986, p. 24). This means disenthralling ourselves from present visions that may have served us for decades. It means looking beyond missions and objectives that already exist and formulating new visions of what the organization might be and do in the future.

We must be careful, however, not to set up a false dichotomy here. Just because events have rendered a purely reactive style obsolete does not mean that leaders should go to the other extreme and unilaterally impose their vision and will on the organization. As noted in the preceding section, there are too many diverse stakeholders, and they are too smart and too well funded and well supported by societal values, for a leader to assume that his or her vision can just be announced and that everyone else (the stakeholders) will then docilely fall in line. Furthermore, in today's complex world, we probably would not even want a situation where a single person was the only source of vision for an organization. There is too great a chance of the vision being wrong, inappropriate for the circumstances, incomplete, out of touch. If a corporation's markets increasingly exist overseas, yet the CEO is not able to personally envision what the international possibilities are, would we not want that person to tap many other perspectives from inside and outside the organization in fashioning a vision? If a university is increasingly acquiring a graduate and professional student body but its president's personal vision is primarily oriented toward the challenge of undergraduate education, would we not want that president to be open to other views (visions) of the institution's future?

An additional danger in heavy reliance on the creative vision of one person can be expressed with the question, where are these people when we need them? The idea of vision is strongly and popularly associated with a single visionary leader who somehow sees what is needed and possible and can inspire others with that vision. We know that there have been thousands of such men and women throughout history. The problem is that we can't call them forth on demand; that is, we can't plan their emergence at the moment in time when they are needed. Because of this association of vision with a single person, it is easy to believe that without one an organization is doomed to mediocrity at best. That need not be the case, but it does leave open the question of how vision can arise in an organization even though there is no single charismatic source. I will have more to say about this later in the chapter.

Even as the day of the purely reactive, firefighting executive is over, so too has the modern world called into question the tradition of the single "man on a white horse" who boldly and charismatically cries "This way!" and then leads the charge. Both sorts of leaders are still around, to be sure, but we cannot limit our discussion of vision to the magic of a single person. With the sophisticated, well-funded stakeholders noted above surrounding and permeating the organization, the *process* of developing and implanting a vision is becoming more and more complicated as time goes on. Yet the *need* for vision continues undiminished.

In the preceding section I described the similarity of the notions of common vision and common purpose. Those who create vision we say are "visioning." In the same sense, we may say that those who articulate purposes are engaged in "purposing," even though the term is not often heard. In Chapter Three, describing what leaders do in high-performing organizations, I defined *purposing* as the continuous stream of actions by an organization's formal leadership that has the effect of inducing clarity, consensus, and commitment regarding the organization's basic purposes. The visions—the vivid and memorable stories, pictures, images, metaphors, slogans, and other symbols—that leaders offer should have the effect of crystallizing a sense of purpose. Vision, in other words, doesn't guarantee a sense of common purpose. A vision could merely entertain people, it could cause fear among them, or it could create conflict among them; it helps to create a common *view* of a given subject but not automatically a common *commitment*. The essential leadership act is to create visions that bring people together and give them a sense of common purpose. It is not any old vision that a leader should be interested in, but rather one that reinforces the kinds of purposes that are needed in the organization in order for it to prosper and fulfill its reason for existing. That explains why David Brown's remark about the executive *wanting* something is so important.

Effective acts of visioning and purposing need not necessarily be elaborate statements. They can be very simple, *if* they convey a mission-relevant message and convey it in a way that everyone can understand. "Nuts!" was General Anthony C. McAuliffe's famous reply to the Nazi ultimatum to surrender at Bastogne. The vision and purpose that the epithet conveys is that surrender is unthinkable. "Threepeat!" was a word that Los Angeles Lakers coach Pat Riley came up with to launch the 1988–89 season after the team had won the professional championship the two previous seasons. Although the team was not successful because of the determination and inspired play of the Detroit Pistons, "Threepeat!" was a guiding image for the Lakers throughout the season. It and General McAuliffe's call are about as vividly compact vision statements as one could ask for. As another example, AMF Inc.—a conglomerate that included Alcort Sailboats, Brunswick bowling equipment, and Spaulding athletic equipment, as well as other recreational products—came up with the phrase "We Make Weekends" as an overarching vision of what the whole company was about.

Interestingly enough, the AMF vision was originally an advertising slogan, but that does not disqualify it as a possible vision statement for other stakeholders, such as employees. One of the most famous examples of a vision aimed at customers that was probably also a powerful motivating influence for employees was Lee Iacocca's personal guarantee in Chrysler TV ads, accompanied by an authoritative slap on the hood of a car: "If you can find a better car built in America, buy it!" Iacocca's proclamation was aimed at Chrysler customers, but it is likely that employees were watching the ad, too. Given that Chrysler was struggling back from the brink of bankruptcy, it may well have fostered pride and hope in them, even as it stimulated demand for the company's cars. It is a powerful vision: "Our boss actually believes we can make it!" Similar corporate slogans that can potentially have a powerful motivating effect on employees might be Weyerhaeuser's description of itself as "the tree-growing company," Du Pont's "Better things for better living through chemistry," an early motto of International Harvester—"Our field is the world," General Electric's well-known "We bring good things to life," and Ford's "Quality is job one."

If—and it is a big if—employees can see these vivid phrases being valued and lived up to in their daily experience of company operations, then the phrases can function as authentic vision statements. However, if employees see the phrases being violated, not only does it make them cynical about the phrases, it becomes less likely that they will believe *any* calls to arms that the organization's leadership offers. The message to corporate leadership is a simple one: Do not proclaim a vision you do not believe in. Do not proclaim a vision just for effect. Be aware that people have a deep need for this sort of inspiration, but that if they become disappointed and cynical, it can be worse than if you had not tried to inspire them with vision in the first place.

One of the most famous vision statements by a corporate leader, which was believed by its creator and which came to galvanize an entire company, was Theodore N. Vail's vision for the original AT&T, enunciated in the 1920s: "We will build a telephone system so that anyone, anywhere in the world, can talk with anyone else, cheaply, quickly, and satisfactorily." This became the Bell System's vision of universal service. It rivals all other organizational visions for the power it came to exert over the thinking and actions of Bell System employees. Perhaps only "Semper Fidelis," the motto of the U.S. Marine Corps, and the "We the People" preamble to the U.S. Constitution could be said to have exerted influence of similar depth.

It is not just the rhetoric, however, for rhetoric is not by itself the act of leadership. Leadership is composed of the combination of clarity and commitment: these two ingredients then make possible the third—consensus. If the top leadership is unclear and uncommitted, it will not be able to foster organization-wide commitment. In the early 1980s, for example, the CEO of one of the nation's largest consumer products companies spoke to his top 100 executives and offered this vision: "We will build the business through providing superior consumer satisfaction and value." This vision occurred on page 1 of a twenty-page prepared text. Its literal meaning was that they would focus on the consumer and that the health of the business (sales, shares of market, profits, and so on) would follow. The remaining nineteen pages never again mentioned the consumer or providing products of the highest quality. The entire remainder of the text was taken up with setting performance targets in terms of increases in sales, shares of market, profit margins, and the like—the "build the business" factors. It is important to understand that a focus on consumer satisfaction and a focus on maximizing financial performance can lead to very different actions by executives. Not surprisingly, people walked out of that meeting quite confused about what the boss really wanted. If there was a vision, it was of a financially successful organization, not one that was willing to do whatever was necessary to provide "superior consumer satisfaction and value."

In short, vision is not rhetoric. Vision may use rhetoric, but it is not the same thing. An example of a relatively nonrhetorical vision is that of Tandem Computers, as envisioned by CEO James Treybig. Treybig expresses his vision in five operating principles, all of which are phrased in a very down-to-earth way (Magnet, 1982, pp. 84 ff.):

1. All people are good.
2. "People," "workers," "company," and "management" are all names for the same thing.
3. Every single person in the company must understand the essence of the business.
4. Every employee must benefit from the economic successes of the business.
5. Management must create an environment where all of the above can happen.

There is a multiplicity to these five statements. They form a collage of meaning. They include ideas about how people are regarded, how they will be treated, what they must understand, and what the leadership responsibility is for making it all happen. Interestingly, Treybig's fifth principle is anticipated in an early list of operating principles of Lincoln Electric Company, arguably the most continuously successful U.S. corporation of the twentieth century. Lincoln has as its fundamental vision the remarkable notion: "A better and better product at a lower and lower price." Lincoln's specific values differ a bit from Treybig's, but it also has on its list, "non-stop repetition by management of the corporate operating philosophy." I stated that purposing generally is a continuous stream of actions by an organization's leadership; Treybig's and Lincoln Electric's insistence that management live the corporate philosophy reflects that definition.

What about the organizational conditions that encourage or discourage the emergence of visionary leaders? I have stated that visionary statements and actions are not purely products of the overwhelming will of single individuals. Do some kinds of organizational conditions make it more likely that a person's or group's vision might come to have meaning in the organization as a whole? Not a great deal is known on this subject, but it is possible to speculate a bit. In Table 4.1, I have listed eight kinds of factors that may influence a person's or group's potential for visionary leadership.

Each of the factors can be viewed as a continuum, the two ends of which are listed. The hypothesis is that the more each factor lies at the "encouraging" end of the continuum, the greater the likelihood that these people or groups will be able to make their visions meaningful to others in the organization. The table helps explain why so many visionary leaders never have the impact in their organization that they would like to have. They may have a powerful personal vision, which may in time be proved dead right, but if too few of the "encouraging" factors in the table are lined up in their favor, they might as well be shouting into the wind.

Table 4.1. Effect on Vision Effectiveness.

Factors Possessed by Potentially Visionary Person or Group	Effect on Vision Effectiveness	
	Encouraging	Discouraging
Credibility with others	High	Low
Positioning relative to the top of the unit in question	At or near	Far from
Relevance of ideas to main mission of unit in question	Clear or close	Unclear or not close
Ability to draw others in	High	Low
Likelihood of long-term commitment to vision	High	Low
Organization members' readiness for new vision	High	Low
Other encouraging factors	Many	Few
Other discouraging factors	Few	Many

The words "unit in question" are used in Table 4.1 to signal that we need not consider only the total organization. We could be talking about a division or department. Vision is needed at all levels of an organization. Although the vision articulated from the very top should encompass the whole, there may well be a need for bringing the overall vision to a sharper focus in specific component units. This is the responsibility of the leadership of those units. Such leaders shouldn't depend on the very top people to provide all the inspiration. Vision doesn't automatically just cascade down the hierarchy; at each level it needs to be revivified by leaders who have thought deeply about what the vision means for them and their people. If the vision from the top is vague or confusing, it is even more important for leaders of component units to take responsibility for clarifying the vision and focusing it on the main mission of the unit.

I draw this section to a close with observations on a subject of great contemporary importance in organizations: *empowerment* (see also Chapter Six). The term embodies a vision that calls for a substantial increase in the influence that lower-level employees will have in an organization that adopts an empowerment philosophy. In the early nineties, it is an idea that many hundreds of organizations in all sectors of society are experimenting with. The surge of interest is due partly to the ideas of so-called Total Quality Management systems, as fathered by W. Edwards Deming and others (Deming, 1986; Juran, 1988); partly to the Malcolm Baldrige National Quality Award's specific support for employee empowerment; partly to excellence guru Tom Peters's emphasis on pushing decision-making authority to the lowest possible level (Peters and Waterman, 1982, chap. 7); and partly to the preparation that research on delegation of authority and on so-called participative management has provided over the past forty years. In other words, it is not as if managers are hearing for the first time about the value of trying to create more autonomy and initiative at lower levels of the organization. Still, empowerment has an appeal, and it has received a commitment from line managers that these earlier concepts never quite achieved.

But what, employees are asking, does empowerment really *mean*? What picture (vision) of life at lower levels of the organization does the word convey? What picture of relationships *between* various levels of the hierarchy does the word convey? Employees everywhere are asking, "Is management really serious?" We can see in empowerment a very important vision that is in the process of being born—or sadly, in many organizations, in the process of becoming an empty promise that does not inspire anyone and in fact may be creating cynicism and resistance. The leadership challenge with empowerment is to "fill out the story" in a way that intrigues, inspires, and excites employees and then quickly begin to take the specific actions that employees will perceive as reinforcing the vision.

Here is a definition of empowerment that I have tried out on several top management teams who say they are committed to the concept:

> Empowerment exists in an organization when lower-level employees feel that they are *expected* to exercise initiative in good faith on behalf of the mission even if it goes outside the bounds of their normal responsibilities, and if their initiative should lead to a mistake—even a serious one—they trust that they will not be arbitrarily penalized for having taken that initiative.

In other words, this definition supports a vision that might be phrased in this way: When you see something that needs to be done, do it! Don't wait to be told to do it, don't sweep the problem under the rug, don't blame it on someone else.

Most of the senior managers who have read this definition are uncomfortable with it. It seems to them to be a license to act irresponsibly. A careful reading will show that it does not encourage that at all, but the point is that it does trigger a *vision* of irresponsible action in the minds of at least some executives who are interested in empowerment philosophy. As one executive vice president of a Fortune 50 company said after reading this definition, "No, that's too extreme. Real empowerment is telling the people what you want from them, giving them the tools to do it, and leaving them alone." Notice what a very different vision of empowerment this is, and notice how much more managerial control it retains compared to the first definition. It leaves management in charge of setting the tasks, determining the relevant tools, and determining the people who will be involved. It also leaves the initiative for communication in management's hands.

The contrast between these two definitions illustrates the problem that a managerial leader faces with any new idea or program. As soon as it is announced, various stakeholders inside and outside the organization begin to envision what it means for them, that is, to see themselves affected in various ways by it. Too many managements forget or underestimate this often feverish visioning that is going on throughout the organization. They don't realize that it is unlikely that clarity, consensus, and commitment will spontaneously and naturally emerge. This is the real meaning of leading with vision: transforming all the various images, hopes, fears, expectations, and desires to contribute toward a way of talking about the organization and its affairs that the majority can commit to.

Making Vision Real

"Each of us sits in a long, dark hall," wrote Herbert Simon, Nobel Prize–winning decision theorist and one of the fathers of organization theory and artificial intelligence, "within a circle of light cast by a small lamp. The lamp light penetrates a few feet up and down the hall, then rapidly attenuates, diluted by the vast darkness of future and past that surrounds it" (Simon, 1981, p. 178). Vision, one might say, is the attempt to extend, even a little bit, Simon's "lamp light" and to provide members of an organization with a feeling for the reality and the significance of what the organization is trying to do. In this section, I turn my attention to some specific things leaders can do to make the vision real for others.

Probably the two most common methods by which leaders make their personal vision real for others are inspirational speech making and personal, intimate conversation with individuals. We see politicians employ such methods constantly, but organizational executives use them effectively as well. Leaders have been making dramatic speeches, filled with vivid and inspiring images, throughout history. Likewise they have been exercising a personal touch with their followers. Shakespeare, for example, has Henry V on the night before the Battle of Agincourt "walking from watch to watch, from tent to tent. . . . That every wretch, pining and pale before,/Beholding him, plucks comfort from his looks." Tom Peters has made MBWA (management by wandering around) a strategic activity for one who would lead toward excellence (Peters and Austin, 1985, chap. 2).

The speech to a large group gives the leader the opportunity to develop the vision in detail, to provide the stories and the metaphors and to link them to the reality that people are experiencing, and to infuse the words and images with personal energy and feeling. By contrast, close-up, one-on-one contact gives the leader the chance to adjust the vision to the particular concerns of individuals; equally important, close contact gives the leader a sense of how people are reacting to the vision. Additionally, it sends a powerful message to everyone that the leader cares enough about the vision to take the time to deliver it personally.

These two tried-and-true methods are still probably the most effective methods that we have. But over the past few decades an additional class of methods has evolved that does not depend so heavily on a single leader having the vision and imparting it either in spellbinding oratory or in the tête-à-tête. We might call these methods *group-centered*, because their essence is that the vision at least partially—and often entirely—grows out of the ideas and vision of organization members, rather than originating with the leader. The leadership that the leader provides is in helping vision to emerge from the members, and it is important leadership indeed. The premise of the many varieties of group-centered approaches is that people support what they have a hand in creating; since vision is so important, the argument goes, the more that people can be part of creating it, the more likely they will be to support it.

On the assumption that speeches and tête-à-têtes are well-understood leadership methods, I will say no more about them here and instead will focus on group-centered methods. It should be noted that in the discussion that follows, we are thinking of a variety of different organizational configurations when we define *group-centered*. The group could consist of the top management of an organization, it could be the leadership of a division of an organization, it could be all members of the organization (although involving more than about one hundred people can get quite unwieldy); it could be two or three groups who are coming together for the first time, as in a corporate merger or reorganization; it could in fact be any set of people who need a common vision.

There are two aspects of group-centered methods, each of which is quite important. The first has to do with the circumstances in which a group of organization members, such as a top executive team, are brought together to engage in joint visioning. The second aspect deals with the specific activities that they engage in to produce a common vision. There is a great deal of quite creative work going on presently in both areas, because both are integral to the emergence of a vision that possesses clarity, consensus, and commitment.

With regard to the first aspect, there is general agreement that the office with its normal modes of conduct is not an effective place for meeting to create a vision. There are too many interruptions, too many competing items on the group's agenda, too many temptations to duck out of the meeting for phone calls or other personal business. Furthermore, the office culture, with its consciousness of roles, responsibilities, and reporting relationships, can get in the way of the egalitarian mood a group needs in order to develop a shared vision. Even such things as the relatively formal attire that pervades most office environments can be a hindrance to the kind of creative thinking that is needed to evolve a common vision. Finally, most office environments do not have the physical spaces and resources that we have learned we need for effective group interaction: open, flexible rooms with lots of wall space, a variety of possible seating configurations, availability of materials with which visual models can be built, and an ambience that invites and stimulates creative thinking. It is quite sobering, in fact, to consider just how much the typical office environment *discourages* collaborative visionary thinking. Perhaps if the modern office had not evolved as a place so unfriendly to visioning work, there would not be so many organizations today that lack a strongly shared vision of who they are and what they can accomplish.

With the office not a felicitous place for visioning work, most organizations have come to make more and more use of retreats or off-site meetings. The conference facilities of commercial hotels have been most often used, but organizations increasingly are building their own facilities. Organizations whose business is to conduct retreats are also springing up. A great deal of innovation is presently going on in the design of learning environments in which visioning work as well as other kinds of creative problem solving can take place. In fact, it is not an exaggeration to say that the design of these settings is becoming so elaborate that there is a danger of a reverse effect occurring where the setting is so self-consciously designed for creativity that participants can't get their minds off it—with the creative work they are there to do correspondingly inhibited!

Closely related to the nature of the setting within which the vision work is to occur are the actual activities that the participants engage in. This is the second key aspect of group-centered methods for generating vision. There has been much experimentation and many innovations. Increasingly, completely worked-out approaches have been developed in which a set of activities has been carefully designed and sequenced and supporting workbooks and software developed. The claim is that a team that goes through the steps under the guidance of a trained workshop leader will end up with a shared vision for its organization. I cannot undertake in this chapter to critique all the various approaches that are proliferating. Instead, I will briefly describe eight kinds of processes that arise with most methods. By implication, we are saying that whether an organization uses a predesigned approach or invents one as it goes along, the following processes can be expected to play an important role in a successful visioning workshop:

1. *Create fruitful interaction.* This includes talking to people in the organization one normally doesn't get to talk to, talking about

things one normally doesn't get to talk about, talking at a more personal level than one often does, and talking in settings, such as mountain hikes or midnight bull sessions, that one usually doesn't share with other organization members.

2. *Create greater team feeling.* This is one result of increased interaction, but it is an objective in its own right. Too often, organization members need to develop greater team feeling and a greater sense of a common fate before it makes sense to generate a common vision. Team feeling is fostered by performing various tasks, often under competitive conditions, that bring people into much closer relations with each other.

3. *Create perspective on organizational issues.* Vision needs to be created from a perspective that is broader than it is usual for members collectively to have. Various exercises get members looking at where the world is going and what roles the organization might play in the emerging conditions. Analysis of the nature and needs of various stakeholders can be carried out in detail. If tradition is important, attention will also be given to where the organization has been and to what these experiences mean for the future. Often members of the organization learn things about the organization and its environment that they have never heard before—both opportunities and threats. The experience is genuinely enlightening and can be a powerful stimulus to clearer vision.

4. *Make leaders accessible.* This is one of the most important benefits of off-site workshops: giving the people in authority an opportunity to show sides of themselves that are hidden by the ordinary office culture. What the boss really thinks about the organization can be a crucial stimulus to vision. Sometimes the boss needs quite a bit of coaching on this matter, because there is a fine line between saying clearly what one thinks and feels and dominating the meeting or suppressing other views. When properly done, though, some reflections from the boss on what she or he sees for the future and wants for the organization can empower people to take risks, say things out loud, or make public commitments that they might otherwise withhold.

5. *Expose and work through conflicts*. Inevitably, any discussion of something as fundamental as the organization's vision will probably produce differences of opinion and often quite pointed conflicts. If these differences aren't recognized and worked through, they will reappear in people's interpretations of the vision itself, and the common commitment that is so important will not be achieved.

6. *Uncover and highlight feelings*. Enthusiasm is not just a frequent by-product of these sessions; it is an essential element. As has been repeatedly said about vision, it is more than just an abstract idea about the organization. It is a personally meaningful picture of what the organization can be, of what its human value can be, and of the role the person who holds the vision can play in helping all this to happen. Enthusiasm, passion, commitment, optimism, a sense of urgency—these feelings are key. If they do not emerge in a workshop devoted to creating vision, it is likely that whatever is being discussed is not very interesting to participants.

7. *Determine next steps and reentry back home*. It is easy to forget in the excitement of visioning that the success of the event depends on what participants take back to the workaday organization, what they tell those who did not attend, what steps they take to begin implementing the vision, and so on. If participants don't spend some time at the workshop talking about this, it is less likely to get done once everyone is back on the job. If a vision is not having much impact on the organization, it is likely that too little attention was given to follow-up work after the vision workshop.

8. *Institutionalize this process for creating and re-creating vision*. One frequently hears participants at these workshops ask, why don't we work this way more often? In other words, the experience does show participants a different way of working. It can give them ideas about ways they might modify their regular organizational culture, and it can give them ideas for future retreats. This is important learning, for there may also be counterforces at work that suggest that a successful off-site vision workshop need never be repeated.

These eight processes arise repeatedly in vision workshops. The first seven are necessary to a successful single event; the eighth factor is needed for an organization to keep its vision fresh and meaningful over time. Highly effective vision workshops will give attention to all eight of these factors. Less successful workshops will ignore or downplay one or more of them.

The role of the organization's leadership in a group-centered process of creating vision is very important. It is the leadership that decides that a group's time on the issue of vision is important, that makes resources available, that models by its own actions the significance of the effort, that uses its visibility and authority to articulate the vision openly and forcefully, that provides "push" and support for subsequent efforts to implement the vision once it has been formulated, that takes on the inevitable cynics and the naysayers. At virtually every step along the way, it is critical that the formal leadership understand and show how important it is to have a vision for which there is clarity, consensus, and commitment. This is an emerging leadership role. As recently as the early 1980s it was hardly understood as a way to exercise leadership. It is a role that has become more and more important as complexity and uncertainty have increased and as more and more stakeholders have sought involvement in the creation of vision for the organization.

The leader's *personal* vision, we might say, is to foster and sustain an organization that possesses vision. This does not mean that the leader plays no role in creating the substantive vision itself, but rather that the leader's own vision needs to actualize *both* the content of the vision *and* the process of making it meaningful to others. In today's turbulent organizational world, leaders who possess only a substantive vision of what the organization should be and do are seriously handicapped, because they will not understand the process by which their ideas can become meaningful to others. They need what might be called a "process vision" of how their substantive ideas and those of others can come to inspire people in the organization. And "process vision" is not too flowery a term, because the process cannot merely be a series of mechanical steps. These vision workshops and other off-site retreats must feel to participants like a good use of time. They must engage and inspire the participants. They must uplift the participants beyond the normal frame of mind adopted for organizational meetings. The various activities participants are asked to undertake must have credibility.

It is not an exaggeration to say that the leadership role in the process of visioning is becoming more important than its role in the actualization of the vision. The latter will always be important, of course, particularly in smaller organizations, but the organizations of the future that achieve and then fulfill their visions will be the ones whose leadership understands the process of visioning.

Special Problems of Vision in Organizations

Enough has been said up to this point for you to realize both how important and how complicated vision is. Leadership with vision is by no means just another management skill. The visioning process can be quite fragile, even in the most well-led and successful organizations. Moreover, because the organizational world is so dynamic, it is unlikely that we will ever solve the problem of vision, making it less elusive. In this final section, I have identified five kinds of special problems that organization leaders can expect will mark the next few years of work on creating and implementing vision in organizations.

1. Multiculturalism and Diversity

All organizations are becoming more demographically heterogeneous (diverse in terms of race, religion, national origin, ethnicity, gender, age, physical ability, and language preference). Multiculturalism and diversity pose challenges to managerial leaders on all fronts because so many of the ideas that we think make up a good organization and a good management are in fact culture-bound. I have addressed this problem at length elsewhere (Vaill, 1989, chap. 10; 1996, chap. 5). Vision is affected by increased heterogeneity quite directly and deeply. I have stated repeatedly in this chapter that the vision needs to appeal to people at the level of their personal need for meaning. Yet the wider the range of their values and experience, the more difficult that is to do. We are at the beginning of understanding what *intercultural* visioning may be like. There is certainly plenty of experience with the failure to achieve a vision that spans culture, as can be seen from the history of racial conflict in North America and the religious conflicts of the Middle East. It is tempting, apparently, to develop a vision that sets your group *against* another group, rather than one that bridges the groups. More and more we are going to see this problem inside organizations as well as in society at large.

2. Loss of Vision

The very rapid pace of technical, economic, and social change has created a situation in which many organizations that once had a clear and powerful vision have lost it. It is doubtful, for example, that the old U.S. Post Office vision with which we began is very meaningful to the current workforce. Theodore N. Vail's vision for AT&T of universal service was also cited. That vision was rendered obsolete by AT&T's divestiture of its operating companies in 1984. Countless other organizations, including some of society's noblest institutions, have seen their vision overtaken by events.

Because of the nature of vision, its loss can be traumatic. Vision is not a mere fact about the organization; it expresses the organization's human meaning and value. When the vision dies, in the eyes of some the organization has died; *they* might as well have died, some may feel. William Bridges has written movingly about the need for people to have time to grieve over the loss of old ways of working and valuing (Bridges, 1988, chap. 3). They cannot be expected to quickly adopt a new vision to go with their changed circumstances. If the psychological significance of the loss of vision is not taken into account, the entire subsequent process of renewal can be affected.

3. The Need for Transforming Vision

In this chapter I have written of vision as something that undergirds all organizational operations. I have not insisted that vision necessarily be heroic or an order of magnitude different from the organization's ordinary mode of operations. However, the rapid rate of change and the increasing turbulence that organizations are living with and will continue to live with are forcing them to produce visions that take them substantially beyond anything they may have done before. They are finding a need to envision a whole new mode of operations—new missions, new customers, new technologies, new ways of acting toward employees and other stakeholders. The word *transformation* has become the popular name for what needs to happen to the thinking of organization members, especially leaders.

Although a great deal of excitement and romance is associated with the idea of organizational transformation, we don't know very much about how to do it (Weisbord, 1987, chap. 14; Owen, 1991). The *vision* of transformation has not yet been fulfilled.

Probably the closest thing to transformation consists of the changes that American corporations have made in response to the Japanese challenge. Such forced changes, however, may be primarily driven by a negative vision, a vision of extinction. The positive view of vision that has been taken in this chapter is much more difficult to come by. This may be an appropriate place to note that the pride the American businessperson seems to take in "running scared" is not actually a very wise strategy for leading an organization: only so much motivation can be squeezed from fear before people either become inured to the alarms or find ways of protecting themselves from the thing that is feared. Leaders who create visions designed to frighten employees into heroic acts are being very shortsighted.

4. Cynicism

Vision is about hope. It involves a measure of trust and a willingness to believe that things can be dramatically better. It involves trusting those who are creating vision—trusting their motives, trusting their moral character. Modern society contains many people who have been bitterly disappointed, by their family, their employer, their government, their friends. Furthermore, there have been many colorful leaders of the past half-century whose visions have not brought the good things that they promised. The developed world has become a society within which it is harder and harder to articulate a vision and be believed; it may even be harder and harder to generate faith within oneself, as discussed in Chapter Eleven. But if vision is to continue to have the inspiring effect that is needed, we have to find ways of combating the doubters and the naysayers.

Integrity has for years been on every list of qualities that executives consider most important. The pervasiveness of doubt and cynicism about vision only underlines the importance of integrity. Leaders should associate themselves only with visions they can put their heart into. To articulate a vision just because the leader thinks the organization needs one is a tragic mistake, for it will only produce more cynicism and despair when the leader's lack of real commitment is revealed.

5. Vision and the Leader's Spiritual Development

I have said that vision deals with fundamental meanings of the organization, that in the turbulent modern environment vision is constantly in need of renewal and revitalization, and that vision must appeal to increasingly diverse groups of stakeholders. Clearly, it would appear that leaders who are going to offer new visions and support others' efforts to do the same need to be men and women of strong character and well-formed personal values. But that is not quite the right way to frame the issue. The leader's character and personal values are not immutable, not the only stable elements in an otherwise totally fluid situation. The leader's values and character are in a process of growth, change, and development. The older view of the leader as the rock on whom everyone leans is being replaced by a view of the leader as the one who demonstrates the *way to be* appropriate for our turbulent days as well as for what our organizations should do. The leader takes the lead in humility, in being a learner—and on the subject of vision the most important area of learning is that of values, priorities, and meanings. People who are learning in these areas have traditionally been seen as being in a process of spiritual growth. Thus, as discussed in Chapter Eleven, executive development is spiritual development when it comes to maintaining an ability to offer a vision that inspires others. There is a growing consensus that learning for leadership needs to occur at this quite personal and profound level of spirituality if a person is to have the resources and the resilience to lead under trying modern conditions.

Conclusion

Our twin themes throughout this chapter have been the nature of vision in organizations and the meaning it has for the work of organizational leadership. Vision is expressive of the feelings held for the organization and its work. Vision is not magic, but it is not exactly logical and clear-cut either. In the short run, an organization can operate on habit and past successes. However, in the longer run, vision is indispensable: it is the basis on which an organization acquires and maintains personal meaning for all those who are associated with it. Vision arises in people who care about the situation they are involved in. The leadership role is to help people *understand* the caring and to express it in terms that will bring them forward into the future.

5

Notes on "Running an Organization"

The comments that follow pertain to any type of purposeful human organization—businesses, government agencies, health systems, educational institutions, voluntary organizations, and so on. These notes are concerned with the education and training of those who are in positions to direct activities in these organizations or subparts of them. These individuals are known variously as *managers*, *executives*, *leaders*, and *supervisors*, as well as by a variety of slang terms such as *bosses* and *head honchos*. I will use the generic term *leader-manager*.

I am ignoring organizational level and job scope in these notes: they could apply to those very high in the organization or to those anywhere in the hierarchy. They could apply to either line or staff jobs. They could apply to a leader-manager who is an unpaid volunteer on some project as much as to one for whom the work is full-time, paid employment. I believe that these observations apply across national and ethnic cultures.

I am assuming two key things as my point of departure. First, the organizational unit in question has some mission and/or objectives or is in the process of formulating them; even if objectives are

---

Note: Originally published in *The Journal of Management Inquiry*, June 1992, 1(2), 130–138. © 1992 Sage Publications, Inc. Reprinted, slightly edited, with permission of Sage Publications, Inc.

implicit, it is understood that this unit exists to *accomplish* something. Second, the leader-manager of the unit is perceived to be one of those accountable for the formulation and accomplishment of these objectives.

Running an Organization

Running an organization means this to me: *repeatedly and successfully exercising influence on others in a dignifying and empowering way on behalf of the variety of objectives, priorities, and constraints existing in the organization, using many different kinds of knowledge, common sense, and skill.* The phrase "running an organization" is deliberately intended to be as nonacademic and nontheoretical as possible. The colloquial meaning of the phrase is the intended one; "getting things done," "making things happen," and "moving things along," are synonymous phrases. The question is, what are we talking about when we use these phrases about a leader-manager in an organization? My definition is a first attempt to answer this question. As we get clearer on what we are talking about, we can move on to the questions of how one learns to do this work and, more specifically, what role formal education and training experiences can play in helping a person develop the ability to run an organization. Because we are talking about variable human beings in variable organizations doing variable work under variable environmental conditions, it is unlikely that there will be any one simple, all-purpose prescription for running an organization. Various scholars over the years have tried to say what the absolute, bottom-line requisite abilities of an effective action taker are. Henry Mintzberg's *The Nature of Managerial Work* (1973), although not the first of the genre, is a relatively recent noteworthy contribution that has spawned virtually a whole academic field of theory and research that I call the "managerial competencies" movement. My perception of all this work, however, is that the overall process of running an organization is being lost in the many distinctions that are being drawn. I am personally quite skeptical about these efforts and have tried to make the case for caution (Vaill, 1989, chap. 2). Running an organization is *not* the sum of a set of competencies.

Loss of Focus

In addition to deliberate research on competencies, we have the various academic disciplines in management schools with their ideas about their own relevance to leading and managing. These disciplines either think that their content is all a leader-manager really needs to know or admit that they are only dealing with a portion of the total range of knowledge and skill required but assume that the rest is being picked up somewhere else in the curriculum. Both of these perceptions tend to be wrong. The first is wrong because of the variety, heterogeneity, concreteness, and change in the leader-manager's job. No single academic field, with its passion for regularities and generalizations, can get its arms around what an individual is doing when running a specific organization. The second is wrong because as each academic field selects its own phenomena from the "buffet" of the actual leader-manager's job, as each academic diner takes what's interesting back to his or her own "table" (that is, courses), no one is giving attention to the job as a whole entity and the person in it as a whole person.

The Myth of the Capstone Experience

Most leader-manager education programs, whether university-based or organization-based, include "integrative" or "capstone" courses and experiences that supposedly give attention to the whole job of the leader-manager and provide an opportunity to temper, refine, and integrate various ideas and techniques. Belief in the efficacy of these capstone experiences is one of the most important myths of our entire educational enterprise. (By *myths* I don't mean lies, but rather the comfortable stories we tell ourselves.) We don't actually study whether capstone courses integrate; we just believe they do. We don't actually experiment very much with various approaches but instead leave it up to individual instructors and trainers.

Many programs rely on the mystique of the Harvard case study to provide data that will test the ability to integrate. In most schools and programs, however, learners have had little prior experience with Harvard-type cases and as a result don't even know how to look at and discuss a case, let alone tease out its "integrative" possibilities. Furthermore, in most schools and programs it is assumed that leading a case discussion is not a particularly difficult instructional skill, and hence most instructors just do it intuitively; again, we don't actually study what these instructors' range of effectiveness is.

A further problem with integrative courses and experiences is that they are increasingly being taken over by faculties who are specialists in strategic management. This is an exciting academic field— one I have participated in actively as a teacher, consultant, and researcher-writer since 1972. But it is not at all the same thing as what I mean by running an organization. In fact, curiously, strategic management downplays *running* an organization as much as or more than any other academic field. It encourages the learner to take an Olympian view of the organization and its situation. It seeks to identify the truly strategic factors that are making a difference. It is primarily cognitive, data-oriented, and verbal in its approach to organizational problems. It looks relatively far into the future to sense issues over the horizon that could be opportunities or threats, but it tends not to concern itself with what is involved in staying the course over the range of time it is considering. It steps over the messiness, contingency, and absurdity of everyday organizational life (although not denying their existence). Strategic management used to ignore organizational culture entirely, which was bad, but now it has decided that organizational culture is a strategic variable to be manipulated as part of the strategy, which is even worse in the sense of being ill informed about the nature of culture. A *culture*, by definition, is not under the control of any member or subgroup of it.

All of these tendencies of strategic management obscure what it takes to run an organization. Furthermore, as the field matures, its specialists become one more set of diners at the buffet of the leader-manager's job, taking back to their table only what they find juicy and delectable.

The Elusive Generalist

From time to time we hear references to someone called the "generalist" as the beau ideal in management. Learners often find these references thrilling. They tap the very deep theme in Western culture of the philosopher king, a theme that goes back at least to Plato. There have always been "big names" at leading business schools who virtually make a career out of describing this generalist. Lots of executive development programs, particularly those put on at leading universities, say or imply that they are training generalists, with the implication that somehow they are therefore higher and grander in their ambitions than programs that just try to train middle managers in nuts-and-bolts management. I find the elitism in these ways of talking suffocating and hardly consistent with the value system a *true* philosopher king or queen would be likely to possess.

Furthermore, all this talk about the generalist tends to obscure what I mean when I talk about running an organization. Not that one doesn't have to be eclectic and flexible and multifaceted to run any organization or piece of it. But actually *leading* and *managing* is so unglamourous and unobtrusive when done well. It is so patient and persistent and pedestrian. It is work in the trenches. The people who really get things done in organizations are *not* seen as philosopher kings or queens! The people who are devoted to running an organization usually do not find time to philosophize about it, romanticize it, make speeches about it, and/or write memoirs about it.

Perhaps this is an appropriate point, also, to note how difficult it is to perform my definition of running an organization successfully.

We're talking about something that can be mentally, physically, and indeed spiritually exhausting, about a life full of contingencies, recalcitrant people, and unpleasant surprises. It is the life that is referred to in the phrases "the loneliness of command" and "You can't please everybody." To be sure, it has the pleasures of major achievements, but running an organization also entails absorbing some painful disappointments and defeats. It is no trade for the fainthearted, the hard-hearted, or the halfhearted, and that is its chief challenge. Men and women, over the centuries, have learned to do this work in the so-called School of Hard Knocks, but the existence of schools of management and of highly organized management development programs implies that we think there might be better ways to prepare people for this life.

Many of us have had the experience as professors of inviting a seasoned executive to class to talk, only to discover that despite the person's accomplishments, he or she may have little capacity to convey in words what it takes. These speakers' focus is frequently just a little "off": the practical stories they can tell tend to be so specific to their industry or product that a listener knowing nothing about it has trouble staying interested, and when they do try to generalize, they often end up with clichés and bits of common sense that the listener finds rather banal. We instructors find ourselves feeding the guests loaded questions and trying to draw them out so the class can see what is special about them. (Fritz Roethlisberger used to say, "There are those who can do it and those who can talk about it. When you find someone who can both do it and talk about it, pay attention!" He was talking about what he called "administrative skill.")

Look again at the definition of running an organization I gave at the beginning of the chapter. That definition is intentionally homely and not intellectually very exciting. If anything, it is *too* academic and self-conscious. That's why I like the phrase "running an organization" better, and why I'll continue to use it. But the definition does capture what we're *not* doing in our nation's management education and development programs. What we're mainly accomplishing is the imparting of *some* of the needed knowledge (but not the common sense or the skill) in our various academic categories, and we're doing it pretty much the way individual instructors feel like doing it. We are imparting this material without reference to the overall job of running the organization, however; indeed, we may be imparting the material in a way that suppresses awareness of the overall activity of running an organization and leads the student to think that possession of knowledge in the head about some managerial action is the same as possession of skill to carry it through. *Skill*, by the way, isn't quite the right word. I am really talking about practical knowledge—knowledge-of-acquaintance, as William James characterized it. Some thinkers on this subject have said it is the difference between the French words *savoir* (knowledge about) and *connaître* (a more personal, intimate kind of knowledge).

I sympathize with the difficulty. How can you make a class sweat over a complex concept or formula or software application while at the same time communicating, "Be aware, however, that we are in a hothouse here. This problem and this algorithm don't look anything like this when they surface in an organization. You won't have the right data, you won't have enough time, key people will think you're crazy and may take steps to prevent this approach, your own energy for this approach may be very mixed, the technique's reputation in the organization may have preceded your use of it and you will have to deal with those stereotypes, the situation may be moving so quickly that by the time you get the problem set up according to the algorithm the need will have passed, there will be others with different, equally sophisticated approaches competing with you," and so on.

It is understandable that if we said all this to a class, someone would stick up her or his hand and ask, "Well, if it's so different in the real world, how come you're making us learn it this way?" Learners *do* wonder, and sometimes they *do* ask, what the class material has to do with the real world of management, and we can expect this to happen more and more as the credibility of the MBA degree declines. When such questions arise, we tend to lamely say something about the inadequacies of the textbook, or the database, or the equipment the university has provided, or we may mumble something about having to crawl before we can walk. We get off the hook of this question somehow. *We don't change our teaching philosophy,* which is to focus on the academic material and to introduce no more of the real-world material than we have to. That's my real concern, I guess. We continue to teach what we know how to teach in management education, continue to let concepts and techniques in our special fields proliferate and pass them on to students, continue to reproduce ourselves in doctoral programs, and continue to avoid the crunch question about how much all this has to do with running an organization.

How the Academy Errs

I think the messiness, contingency, sprawl, and, indeed, danger of the real managerial world ought to be the *centerpiece* of our thinking, not an afterthought, not a concession to learners' questions like the one above, not something we find amusing or annoying. I think that to the extent that we can't face up to what it takes to run an organization we shouldn't be taking the student's money, because I think that's what most of them are hoping to learn, even though they might not be able to articulate it. I am absolutely not quarreling with our intrinsic interest in our fields, our belief in their validity, or indeed our perception of their beauty. I *am* suggesting that these qualities are not necessarily educational for running an organization.

None of our academic specialties is really about my definition of running an organization. It seems clear to me that no single academic or professional discipline encompasses what is involved in running an organization, nor, I think, can there be one that does. In its essence, the real managerial job transcends the scope of any academic field. The managerial job is basically unbounded: you deal with whatever you have to deal with in order to fulfill objectives and stay within constraints.

We academic specialists—even the most eclectic of us—tend to bound ourselves. We are very concerned, even obsessed, with being able to say what we are about. Our obsession leads us to create categorical schemes concerning what our fields are and are not about. Then begins all the skirmishing among fields that we know so well as we vie with each other for various pieces of content that we think belong in "our" field. This is how we lose sight of the whole person doing the whole job of running the organization. My best guess is that we began to lose focus in the early 1960s. Around that time, the famous Ford Foundation and Carnegie Foundation assessments of business education called for strengthened subject matter. The assumption was that higher-quality subject matter would lead to higher-quality education for managing (that is, for running an organization). It didn't happen. We did get higher-quality subject matter; oh boy, did we. All management school faculty are today far more technically proficient than our counterparts of twenty-five years ago. But do we know more as people about running an organization? And are we doing more as educators to help students learn about running an organization? I think the answer is no to both questions. In fact, I think we have lost ground on these two questions.

From time to time, in the best tradition of academic freedom, individuals among us do orchestrate events in our classes and programs that emphasize actually running an organization. However, these individual efforts, being occasional and affecting only some students, do not alter the overall curriculum. Those who try such experiments feel unappreciated by their colleagues for these efforts. They can usually point to a host of ways the institution uses to discourage them from going outside the academic frame—outside the classroom, outside the academic clock and calendar and grading system, outside academic standards for instructor qualifications, outside acceptable standards for books and other materials. Innovations that try to make running an organization more real for students are in fact exhausting within the present system and it is no wonder that few if any of them last long enough to become a regular part of the curriculum.

These sporadic innovations affect only a few students and involve only a few faculty, many of whom have become quite dispirited about ever making management education more real. Unless we are willing to change, we should stop pretending that what we are doing as an institution meets the objective of helping young men and women learn to run an organization. I don't know of a school of management or a department of management training and development that I would exempt from this statement.

Five Principles

If we made the messiness, contingency, sprawl, and danger of the real managerial world the centerpiece of our efforts rather than an afterthought or a concession, what would we do differently? Maybe it's just in the nature of the academic beast to contort any subject beyond all recognition. Maybe we should rely on other forces at large in the world to correct for our excesses and add the mentalities and abilities we are failing so completely to impart. There may be considerable merit to this position, especially as managing an organization does indeed call for more and more technical knowledge. However, I'm not ready to give in on this question. I still think there is value in discussing how much more we might be doing to regain a focus on running an organization. To that end, I offer the following thoughts.

There are at least five broad principles that I think should suffuse any degree program or training program that purports to be about leading and managing organizations. Let me emphasize that in my mind these five principles should suffuse every program element, no matter how narrow or technical or broad and philosophical, and if an instructor either can't or won't work to keep these principles alive for the learner, he or she shouldn't be permitted to continue.

1. Preserve the Wholeness of the Leader-Manager Job

It's either tragic or amusing that throughout management education, we manage to ignore the meaning of the phrase "common body of knowledge" (CBK). That is a phrase from the BBA/MBA accreditation standards of the American Assembly of Collegiate Schools of Business. The CBK has existed in substantially unaltered form for over thirty years. It spells out what business basics every student should be familiar with. Counterpart CBKs exist in accreditation standards in public administration and health services administration as well as in other fields. However, very few schools actually teach the basics as a *body*, that is, as a system of interrelated elements; with a common body in a given business school, every student would get pretty much the same system. In other words, a school would actually have a philosophy, a point of view about the leader-manager job. Students would realize that they had something in common; they might even feel like fellow professionals, a cadre. Faculty members, too, would share this point of view and reinforce each other's research and theorizing about it.

In my opinion, this body is still right there in front of us to address. The trouble is that as long as we restrict ourselves to a collection of three-credit courses taught by various loosely acquainted faculty members, none of whom consider the basic course their real academic interest, with no controls on room quality, teaching materials, timing, or sequencing of experiences, we will never achieve an educational program that imparts a sense of the body. If we could do a powerful job on the common body, I would be willing to let students take any further specialized courses that they wanted. Specialized courses would not expunge the awareness achieved in the common-body course (note the singular) of the wholeness of the leader-manager job.

2. Preserve the Time or Process Quality
of the Leader-Manager Job

Time and process are relatively neglected aspects of research on the leader-manager job, yet people in these jobs are fundamentally building organizational capabilities and relationships through time. The temporality of the leader-manager job is elusive, which may explain why it has been neglected, but if we're interested in strengthening a program's focus on running an organization, it has to be emphasized (Vaill, 1998).

It is very hard in the classroom to help the learner see the importance of drive and persistence and patience in effective leading and managing. We know there's a difference in awareness of the organizational culture between a person who has had six months in a job and one with five years in it. We know that follow-up is one of the most important qualities a manager can possess, even though academia has overlooked it entirely. We know that a vision may require years of effort to bring to fruition. We know that implementing *any* course of action involving *any* academic subject matter calls for a feel for timing and pacing, and that this "feel" is often what brash, "instant gratification" MBAs most notably lack in their first years on the job (see also principle 3 below).

Things we might do to preserve the time or process quality include (a) giving the learners longitudinal (instead of "snapshot") cases and other research studies that show organizational processes through time; (b) bringing in outside speakers who have been using the ideas and techniques contained in a course for a number of years to discuss how they look, feel, and operate not as one-shot techniques but as matters of continuing practice and emphasis; (c) creating exercises that help learners both understand and stretch their time horizons; and (d) creating themes that run through the curriculum of a program to help learners experience their *evolving* understanding, rather than thinking in limited, modular terms where one "takes" a course and then moves on to something else.

3. Preserve Feeling in the Leader-Manager Job

I do not mean "feeling" as in the unfortunately demeaning "touchy-feely" label that has gotten tacked onto the aspects of the job that have to do with working closely with people. Having respect for people and the ability to work effectively with them is of course important. But the principle of preserving the feeling in the job as we present it to learners is what I think the great theorist Chester Barnard meant when he said that true executive abilities are matters of "feeling, judgment, sense, proportion, balance, appropriateness" (Barnard, 1938, p. 235). These qualities go beyond having logical reasons for one's actions.

Management education has become almost exclusively rationalistic in the past thirty years. Perhaps it has always tended to move in this direction and our inability to convey the part played by human qualities other than purely cognitive-rational ones is one of our biggest failings in management education. The temptation with this question, of course, is to set up a false dichotomy: "*Either* we treat leading and managing rationalistically *or* we treat it as an irrational power struggle governed by who can shout the loudest and manipulate the most cleverly." In my view, there have to be other alternatives than these two stark choices, for neither one is very attractive. My perception is that the rationalistic approach is overwhelmingly dominant in all subject matter areas, including my own field of organizational behavior.

The essence of the rationalistic approach is to insist that a leader-manager consciously and logically think through both the causes of problems, the remedial alternatives available, the criteria for choosing among them, and the implementation plan by which the chosen alternative will be installed. As we know, an enormous number of concepts and analytical techniques have grown up to support this implicit injunction that a manager must have good, conscious reasons for everything he or she does. The trendy word is *accountability*: one must be able to account for all of one's actions— so the rationalistic argument goes.

I am using *feeling* for a mode of knowing that is not irrational but at the same time may not meet the strictest criteria of logic and completeness. The process by which we get clear on something, by which we "see what needs to be done," by which we develop a sense of pacing and timing (see principle 2 above) is something familiar to us all, I hope. In very complex, very fast-moving situations, we *depend* on these abilities. We don't know much about exactly how they can be developed and strengthened, but I certainly think any management program is deficient that does not recognize the reality of these abilities in leadership and management.

One of the reasons that effective leading and managing is so hard to understand is that we keep asking for logical reasons to explain why people comply with and commit themselves to the leader-manager's projects. We often seem not to realize that it is in feelings such as loyalty, admiration, respect, and affection that leader-managers bridge themselves to others, not just at the level of the facts. We know that a course of action has to make sense to someone; merely making sense in abstract logic is not enough, especially when a person is going to have to take substantial risks and/or devote considerable time to the project.

Preserving the feeling in leading and managing should lead us to place more emphasis on the qualities of character that our learners need to possess. Some will say, "You can't teach values and character." I respond, "Yes, but can they be learned?" because if the answer to that is even a qualified yes, then it seems to me that the challenge is before us to find ways of showing learners how important a sound character is in effective leading and managing, and of suggesting things they might do to develop on this dimension. Again, my concern is with our consistent tendency to overlook this whole area, rather than with prescribing one best way to deal with it.

4. Preserve Initiative in the Leader-Manager Job

It seems to me that all our rationalistic talk about the importance of objectives has obscured something of great importance: the leader *leads*. Within MBA education over the past thirty years a rather distressing tendency has grown up to take the existence of the organization, its mission and major objectives, as relatively given, as mysteriously already present in the situation. The majority of our MBAs graduate with a mentality that says, "I am now supposed to go to work for someone and practice my functional specialty, my 'major,' in the context of that employment." The equivalent mentality for graduates of in-house training programs is that they are to take the skills the program has imparted and apply them to situations that occur on the job.

This mentality is not consistent with what it takes to run an organization. The person who is running the organization (including a subpart if that is all the person is responsible for) is focusing on achieving objectives that are personally important to him or her and on coping with problems that arise in pursuit of those objectives. The focus is not on the skills—it is on what one is trying to get done. Real initiators are not merely presiding over the organization and they are not just passively facilitating others' pursuit of objectives. What we are failing to impart is a mentality of shaping the organization and disciplining it and its members toward objectives that are felt as desirable values. We academics can afford to conceptualize objectives as logical elements in a course of action, but for those involved, embedded, entangled in the organization, objectives have to be personally desirable values, for otherwise they will be abandoned the minute the going gets tough.

We don't tell our graduates about the importance of going to work for an employer whose mission they love and respect. We don't spend much time stressing how there has to be some agreement between what the system needs and what they as its leaders personally want. We leave them with one of the most unfortunate impressions any graduate from a school of managing and leading can receive—that there are organizational objectives and then there are personal career objectives, *and there need be no particular correspondence between the two*. Too many of our graduates end up in jobs where they can treat objectives as just what they always were in their classes: rather remote, abstract formalities—not matters of impassioned commitment. The only objectives they treat as real are the immediate functional objectives in connection with the specialized technical work they are doing. We haven't been educating and training our learners to take initiative on behalf of the mission of the system. We're producing system operators, not system builders.

This tragic split helps explain why there are so many organizational problems that no one is doing anything about. If they don't happen to be interesting to someone, nothing is done about them. A particular deficiency in this area is the number of organizations that are presently in need of leadership on their basic mission and strategic objectives. It turns out that many, many organizational leaders have little idea how to take the lead on a new mission, although since the publication of Peters and Waterman's (1982) book everyone is talking about the subject. They have created a wonderfully remunerative consulting market, but that doesn't alter the fact that a very large number of executives are not sure how to proceed with a basic reformulation of mission and strategy. It is as if no one told these executives about the fundamental, personal shaping of people's thinking that they might have to do. Right when their personal leadership is most needed, many of them get a sudden attack of remoteness, a sudden interest in a conference a long way from home, a sudden availability for a new position in another organization.

5. Preserve the Humanism in the Leader-Manager Job

It is not often noted that you can't lead money or equipment or a computer or even a market or an organization, for these are all non-human abstractions. You can only lead people. Furthermore, my own opinion is that you don't lead people by applying behavioral science *to* them. Something else is involved, something we have not consistently identified and achieved in our educational philosophy about leadership and management.

The closest that I can come to it is to say that the leader-manager is a *moral agent,* a moral agent who is trying to do good for others. This image has been appropriate as long as there have been leaders and managers, that is, long before there were any academic fields or any degree programs. Leaders and managers try to do the right thing in terms of their own values and in terms of the organizational needs they can perceive. Not only do *they* try; those around them hold them responsible for trying and expect them to try to do good. From both points of view, that of the "sender" and that of the "receiver," the moral agency of leaders and managers is accepted. So why isn't the moral philosophy of leadership and management the center of our concern as educators and trainers? I have no desire to see us march in lockstep and become doctrinaire on the matter, but why don't we even *discuss* it among ourselves and with our learners? Why do we translate what I'm talking about into something we call business ethics and then offer it as, at most, an elective, an elective that we water down into a subject we want the learner to know about rather than a fundamental matter of character on which will hinge the learner's long-run value as a leader and manager, and probably her or his mental and spiritual health as well?

Even though there has been a recent resurgence of interest in the subject of ethics among some educators, I don't think it is an exaggeration to say that the vast majority of us have little or no interest in the question of the moral awareness and moral maturity of our learners. I think this is—there is no other word—a scandal. We have access directly and through our learners to enormous economic and political power around the world. We are affecting the moral consciousness of the global society of the future to a degree matched by no other set of educators. Despite our private sensibilities, we seem not to believe that the moral consciousness of our learners is a particularly important question. We are indifferent to this responsibility; indeed, we are for the most part skeptical and resistant to the idea that we even possess it.

We deflect tirades like this one of mine by responding, "What do you suggest?" What I might suggest is not the point, for I am talking about the absence of institutional interest in the question. What any single educator might suggest—and, of course, there have been many clarion calls over the years—is blanked out by the frame we place on the leader-manager job, a frame that excludes moral agency entirely or relegates it to "just another way of talking about the role."

If we don't face the fact that education and training for leadership and management—including *everything we think we should be teaching*—is about values and standards and morals and is a modern-day pursuit of the ancient dream of the good, we truly are just rearranging the deck chairs on the *Titanic*. We will be turning over the organization to what Princeton anthropologist Melvin Tumin once called the law of least morality, which says that the moral level of any group or organization will sink to the level of the least moral member (Tumin, 1964). Our graduates will either *be* the least moral member or will be that member's victim. The possibility that these predictions are already occurring troubles me greatly and provides the chief motivation for these notes.

A Conclusion and a Challenge

These five areas of emphasis should suffuse our curriculum. I am less concerned with any specific content that we might think is appropriate than I am with reforming our view of what we're doing and of why our curriculum exists in the first place. Without more clarity, consensus, and commitment at the level of who we think the professional we're developing is, management education and development will continue to proliferate as a Christmas tree of loosely related courses and experiences held together by nothing more than the assumption by learners that having advanced education and training in management and leadership is probably a good thing to do. This assumption is increasingly coming into question. If increasingly large numbers of learners actually need to be convinced that all the time and effort is worth it, what response do most schools have? Basically, what they have is a bunch of comfortable slogans from the 1950s and 1960s and some claims but no data on the significance of their subject matter for future leaders.

At the present time, most management schools do not have any data (except perhaps some spotty placement statistics on recent graduates) to show that they are accomplishing anything. Meanwhile, the accrediting agencies are getting interested in "output measures" and are gradually reforming evaluation criteria in this direction. *If a school is going to be judged by output measures, it has to have some idea of what it is trying to accomplish in the first place.* This goes well beyond just spelling out a mission statement and a few verbal objectives that split the difference between various faculty interests and specialties.

The main way that schools are going to develop more clarity and consensus and commitment to their missions is through the leadership of their deans, department chairs, and key program administrators. These individuals need the mentality and skills that go with effectively running an organization. Ironically, there is not much interest in these kinds of skills in academia or in other professional organizations that deliver management education and training. Faculty members do not like the connotations that go with being a member of an organization that someone is "running." Consulting and training firms are notoriously badly run. Yet interestingly, every significant educational experiment in management and leadership of the last fifty years has had at its core one person or a small team who knew how to get things done and, in particular, who knew how to get major change implemented.

It is a tautology to say that good things get done in organizations because there are people present who possess the core ability to get things done. To this I respond, "Just so; a tautology it is." How is it, then, that we are managing to conduct this whole enterprise of management education and development with so little attention to this core ability?

Part III

Learning

6

The Learning Challenges of Leadership

This chapter is concerned with the learning challenges of organizational leadership. The objective is to show what these challenges are, to offer a more general way of thinking about learning challenges, and to apply what has been said to a particular leadership topic, that of empowerment. A case is made for the importance of learning as a foundational element in effective leadership. The importance of these matters is created by the exceedingly turbulent and unpredictable organizational environments within which managerial leaders are working. These environments are rendering all statements about what leadership is and what leaders do moot. Leadership, I will argue, is mainly learning.

The Content of Contemporary Leadership

There is basically no limit to the kinds of learning a contemporary organization leader may have to engage in. It is hardly an exaggeration to say that sooner or later, every organization has to deal with

Note: Presented at the Annual Meeting of the American Psychological Association, Toronto, Canada, August 12, 1996. Published as a chapter in E. P. Hollander and L. R. Offermann (eds.), *The Balance of Leadership and Followership*. College Park, Md.: Kellogg Leadership Studies Project, University of Maryland, 1997. Reprinted with permission of publisher.

every other kind of organization and stakeholder that there is. No longer, if it was ever true, can a business just expect to deal with businesses in its primary industry and with a known and stable set of suppliers and customers. The "public interest," with which a government agency is concerned, is an increasingly heterogeneous collection of organizations, individuals, and other entities—all with differing missions, core technologies, operating structures, and work content. Health systems, voluntary organizations, educational institutions, professional services firms—they too are finding that in order to pursue their own missions they have to be knowledgeable about an extraordinary range of issues, trends, and opportunities in their environment. Furthermore, all this variety is itself in a process of continual change and evolution in unpredictable directions. One need only contemplate the significance for any organization of three such diverse trends as the Internet, multiculturalism, and the collapse of the Communist bloc: with relatively little warning to ordinary civilians, these three trends broke across the organizational world with great speed, complexity, and impact. Managerial leaders could do nothing but attempt to learn as best they could the significance of events such as these for their organization and its future.

I have used the metaphor of "permanent white water" to capture the idea of opportunity mixed with danger amid constant turbulence, which is the world of today's organization leaders (Vaill, 1989, 1996). Permanent white water is a continual, disorderly procession of surprising, novel, ill-structured events that demand a leader's learning, with high costs for inattention or misinterpretation.

I have come to think, though, that even the metaphor of a wild river does not adequately capture the reality that managerial leaders are facing. They are not just attempting to survive the shocks and surprises that are buffeting them and their organization. They are trying to be proactive at the same time, pursuing intended changes in products, services, cost structures, technologies, and organizational structures and cultures and, beyond these, seeking a transformative change of their basic mission and purpose. It is the planning and conduct of intended changes within a highly turbulent field of uncontrolled and frequently unanticipated change that is the reality for today's managerial leaders. The wild river cascades in all directions.

The Learning Premise and the Reflective Beginner

More facts and concepts could be advanced to buttress the view of contemporary managerial leadership suggested above. There are variations by type of organization, of course, by industry, by technology, and by the particular mission an organization is pursuing. Society tries to protect some organizations, such as educational and religious institutions, from the shocks and dangers of the modern environment. However, I am convinced after considerable exposure to a wide variety of organizations that all managerial leaders are feeling a dramatic quickening in the pace of change, an increasing complexity to their choices, and a greater and greater cost of being wrong. "Betting the company" is a phrase whose significance is real for managerial leaders of all kinds.

Reference was made in the previous section to the continual stream of things managers have to learn in order to survive in this environment. The amount and variety of such learning is, in fact, so great that it suggests a new kind of generalization about what managerial leadership is. The prevailing and relatively unexamined assumption of our management schools and our management development programs is that managerial leadership is something that is learned. On the contrary, I think it may make more sense to say that in the present world, managerial leadership is not learned; it is learning. That is its essence. That is what we are looking at as we observe a managerial leader at work—a learning process, an exceedingly complex learning process.

We are looking at a human being facing in real time a condition that is problematic for the organizational objectives the person is pursuing. The objectives themselves may be changing, and the problematic condition may be changing as well. The person's intent is to understand this evolving problem well enough so that human, financial, and physical resources—themselves undergoing various kinds of unpredictable and barely controllable change—can be organized and mobilized (that is, led) to address the problem; all this is going on day after day, year after year, in connection with everything the person gets involved in. Of course many different attitudes and abilities come into play in this process. But learning abilities pervade the process. They are of primary importance, because on them depend the person's ability to adapt whatever other behavioral skills he or she possesses to the evolving situation. *Managerial leadership in this view is never really learned; it is ongoing learning.*

I call this assertion the "learning premise." It is a different point of departure for thinking about the nature of managerial leadership. To be immersed in a learning process—to be proceeding from the learning premise—is to be continually confronted with newness— new problems, ideas, techniques, concepts; new gestalts; new possibilities and new limits; new awarenesses and understandings of oneself. Learning also means reinterpreting things already understood and letting go of former understandings and techniques, even if at the level of brain physiology one never literally "unlearns."

To be immersed in newness is to feel like a beginner. What is the psychology of the beginner, particularly of the adult as a beginner? Permanent white water makes this an urgent question, especially since the culture of the developed world is much more preoccupied with competence and mastery than it is in "beginnerhood." (Perhaps it is permanent white water itself that feeds our preoccupation with competence and mastery. How else explain our willingness to believe that an existentially qualitative Olympic gymnastic performance can be validly scored to three decimal places?) What can it possibly mean to attain competence if that competence depends on continual learning in a world of permanent white water?

However, in the modern managerial culture one should know what one is doing. Leaders especially are expected to proceed smartly and confidently. Beginners are new kids on the block, just finding their way around (in a daze), rookies, freshmen, people who don't know which end is up, who have to have their noses wiped and things explained to them in words of one syllable. A beginner is the Wrong Thing to Be, even if it is in fact the case on issue after issue for someone who ostensibly bears the responsibility of leadership. Thus we have a rather profound conundrum: the culture has trained us not to like ourselves or each other very much as beginners, yet permanent white water makes beginners of us all.

The whole question of the psychology of the adult beginner is too large a subject for this chapter. However, the nature of "beginning," in and of itself, is clearly an important part of the larger subject. Beginning is some little-understood compound of self-awareness and situational perception. The learner I am particularly interested in (a managerial leader) is one who realizes, however reluctantly, that the *role* requires learning: it is not a leisurely "when I get around to it" kind of learning, not an avocation, not a casual encounter. Can we begin to picture what a managerial leader in white water on all sides is actually doing as he or she confronts something never experienced before? As the managerial leader experiences beginnerhood repeatedly, *perhaps she or he begins to learn how to become a beginner.*

The Idea of a Learning Challenge

A thorough analysis of what it means to become a better and better beginner is beyond the scope of this chapter. However, a key element in the process is learning to understand more and more clearly the learning challenges that inhere in a particular subject. As one begins learning anything, the peculiar learning opportunities and difficulties of that subject emerge. Most of us have not been taught anything systematic about identifying learning challenges. Some teachers have intuitively identified particular learning challenges and adapted their presentation of material to minimize those difficulties. Much more rarely, I suspect, do teachers take the time to point out learning challenges in a subject, and only very rarely would a teacher take time to help learners understand the nature of learning challenges in general.

What might be some generic characteristics of learning challenges? Here is a brainstormed list of some possible characteristics of a subject that we can say constitute "learning challenges" in the sense that they will affect a learner's ability to learn. A particular subject may be more difficult and frustrating to learn if it possesses one or more of these characteristics:

- Sheer intellectual complexity of content, including the amount of prior learning that is prerequisite to the present content

- Dynamic content that is changing rapidly due to ongoing research and/or the continual emergence of new issues and applications

- Controversy among experts about the importance of the content, its basic nature, the appropriate process for learning it, and so forth

- Dissimilarities between the learning challenges of the present subject and the learner's prior experience

- Relative "nondecomposability" of the subject; difficulty with breaking it into elements without substantial distortion

- An important social dimension to the learning process, as with team sports and many of the performing arts, where learning must occur in concert with the learning of others

- The requirement that learning occur in specialized times and places

- Relatively long delays in receiving positive feedback regarding one's progress, as in playing golf or the violin

- The need for substantial changes in personal style and mentality, for example, the need to adopt a "professional attitude," in order for the content to be understood and practiced effectively

- Lack of contemporary models and exemplars that show the learner what high-quality knowledge of and ability with the subject look like

- A substantial component of arbitrary doctrine or technique, whose significance is unclear, that must be simply accepted and learned on faith

- High dollar cost or other forms of substantial cost, including the cost of other opportunities forgone

- Proprietary barriers such as membership in a particular organization or possession of relatively inaccessible tools or information

- The cultural significance of the content, especially the possibility that this learning will impair the learner's relationships with significant others

No doubt other generic learning challenges could be added to this list, and particular subjects may possess idiosyncratic learning challenges of major importance to the learner. Moreover, we need a more systematic theory of learning challenges, rather than just a list of characteristics. For the moment, though, I will assume that you can infer how the items on this list might affect learning, although it obviously remains to spell out the possible effects in more detail and also to begin investigating these effects empirically.

I have said in several different forums that I am not sure of the extent to which these generic challenges are news. It is possible that learning theorists have already investigated these matters thoroughly. My main point in including them in a discussion of leadership is that I have not heard anything like these characteristics discussed among leadership educators. Perhaps that reveals an unfortunate personal insularity, but so be it. In thousands of hours of discussion of leadership education for more than three decades, I have never heard anyone discuss in systematic terms the learning challenges of leadership. If what I have called the learning premise is accurate, it is time to think more thoroughly about the learning challenges of leadership. And even more importantly, it is time to begin introducing these challenges to leadership learners (or "leaderly learners," as I believe it is more grammatically correct to call them [see Vaill, 1996, chap. 4]).

All of the problems organization leaders are facing contain complex learning challenges. The Internet, globalization, and the collapse of the Communist bloc were mentioned earlier. An analysis of the learning challenges these phenomena present would be sobering. Total Quality Management is a topic containing many interesting learning challenges, not the least of which is a statistical basis that goes far beyond the knowledge of most managers. The downsizing revolution has been an agonizing one, partly because the lessons of humane downsizing are so difficult to learn in the midst of all the pressure to just get it done. In principle, there is no limit to the topics containing complex learning challenges for managerial leaders. Thorough and extended treatment of the whole matter is clearly needed.

For the moment, though, let us focus on one particular learning challenge for managerial leaders that has been receiving a great deal of attention in the 1990s, namely, the topic of empowerment.

The Learning Challenges of Empowerment

With the idea of learning challenges in hand and a sense of the variety of learning challenges that arise constantly for today's organization leaders, we can ask, how might these ideas apply to the learning process of empowerment? In general, with the idea of empowerment we are talking about ways of acting by leaders that result in more initiative and responsibility being taken by subordinates or "followers," more willingness by leaders to take risks and make mistakes, less preoccupation with clearing everything "up the line" before acting.

In an early example of what today we would call an empowerment philosophy, TRW Systems (formerly Space Technology Lab-
oratories) of Redondo Beach, California, had as an operating
principle in the 1960s, "Responsibility must always exceed authority," thus standing on its head one of the most cherished of the traditional management principles: "Responsibility must never exceed
authority." As it was explained to me at the time, this meant, "If
you see something that needs doing, do it. Don't wait for the
bureaucracy to catch up. In the fast-moving aerospace environment,
the opportunity may well have passed if you wait for clearance from
upper management." Of course, the sheer existence of the principle did not automatically mean that TRW managers consistently
and successfully empowered their people, but at least this example
shows the lines along which the company was thinking and is of
historical interest.

The empowerment idea is not a new one. Its spirit and intent
were expressed earlier under the rubrics of participative management, management by objectives, and even delegation of authority.
Driving decision-making authority to the lowest possible level was
one of Tom Peters's original eight principles by which excellent
companies manage themselves (Peters and Waterman, 1982). However, the challenge of successful empowerment is ever new. As discussed above, changes in personnel, technology, markets and other
environmental forces, and turnover of leadership itself mean that
the problem of empowerment is never finally solved. It is an example of what Warren Bennis once called a "predicament" rather than
a problem to be solved (personal communication, May 1977). The
challenge of empowerment arises over and over again in different
guises. This makes the process of empowering subordinates a continual learning process for a leader rather than a definitive action
that, once decided, then becomes a given for that group of leader
and followers.

Let us attempt to be a bit more systematic about the learning
challenges of empowerment. If we picture a leader with a given set
of followers and in a given set of circumstances, attempting to act

in such a way that the followers become noticeably more willing to take initiative and exercise unsupervised responsibility, what can we hypothesize that this leader will be having to learn as he or she proceeds?

Perhaps the most basic learning challenge is embedded in the givens of the preceding paragraph, that is, *the leader will need to learn the meaning of empowerment to these learners in this context*. The leader's empowering actions have to make sense to these specific people in this specific context. Empowering behavior is very probably not generally acceptable behavior—behavior that works most of the time—especially in today's organizational contexts of performance pressure, competition, and threat. Followers need very good reasons to take the increased initiative empowerment intends; they need to trust that the leader's actions mean what they seem to mean. They need to feel that the leader's actions are in support of them as individuals.

From this point about how contextual empowering behavior will be, another learning challenge follows, namely, that *empowerment results from the learning of both leader and followers*. Empowerment cannot be the learning process of a single person; it is a mutual learning process of the leader learning about the followers and the followers learning about the leader. A direct implication of the interactive nature of empowerment learning is that little if any empowering behavior can be learned "off-line" in an artificial situation devoid of the followers and other situational factors with which a leader's behavior is going to interact. (This point about the interactive nature of leadership learning is probably true for most of the key behaviors in leadership. This accords with the intuition so many have had that leadership cannot be learned in a classroom.)

The interactive nature of empowerment learning means that *empowerment learning requires a leader to become much more involved with followers and/or subordinates*. In the fast-paced environment of modern organizations, with people out of the office as much as or more than they are in and fleeting relationships the order of the day, deeper interpersonal involvement itself is a major learning chal-lenge. Such involvement is increasingly difficult physically, to say nothing of its psychological difficulties. Empathy is not a product of fleeting contact, but it is required in order to understand whether the other person is truly feeling more empowered as a result of things one has said and done.

Inevitably, another learning challenge arises: *much of a leader's learning about empowerment may be learning about the various ways in which she or he has heretofore acted in a thoroughly disempowering way.* This realization led me some years ago to coin the term "nondis-empowering" to describe the behavior of someone who has learned how to stop acting in a disempowering way toward followers and subordinates. Nondisempowerment may be especially important learning for a leader who has been functioning in a hierarchical organization and/or a society heavily stratified by social class. The behaviors, learned over many years, that come naturally to a leader in such conditions have the effect of preventing or suppressing (some might say "oppressing") the very actions by followers and sub-ordinates that we would call empowered. It is also important to note that heavily stratified systems train and indoctrinate subordinates in remaining disempowered. For them, learning to seek and accept empowerment—a process that has been called "consciousness rais-ing"—can be difficult and painful.

Learning to be more nondisempowering involves learning many new actions that are more supportive and facilitative. For many lead-ers this means becoming able to give up control. A considerable amount of stress and anxiety may go with this learning, so *handling the anxiety that goes with learning to relinquish control is itself a major learning challenge for empowerment.* Steven Rhinesmith, a well-known organization development consultant who focuses on intercultural relations, has said, "There is no way to create significant change unless you are willing to let things get more out of control than you are comfortable with" (presentation to a conference of the Col-lege Consortium for International Studies, Washington, D.C., Feb-ruary 10, 1996). Rhinesmith's remark crystallizes one of the deepest learning challenges of empowerment, a challenge that those urging leaders to empower followers may underestimate. Even a leader who personally believes in the philosophy of empowerment is likely to feel vulnerable under the crushing performance pressures that contemporary leaders are experiencing in modern organizations.

An almost poignant special case of the problem of relinquishing control is found in many organizations where the leader is the leader because he or she possesses substantially more technical ability and experience than followers and subordinates. This technical ability may need to be placed in suspension in favor of the contributions of others. Understandably in such circumstances, *the learning challenge is in reconceiving and learning to express one's technical ability differently so that room is created for the technical contributions of others*.

Greater involvement with followers and more shared control with them in how things go in the organization brings with it learning challenges of ethics and morality. Empowerment means that the leader is no longer the sole or even the primary source of the ethical quality of decisions and actions. One of the oldest principles of management is that authority can be delegated but responsibility cannot. The more thoroughly a philosophy of empowerment is implemented, the more this principle is put to the test. The same leader who is perfectly willing to "take the heat" for her or his own decisions and actions may be sorely tempted to lay the heat onto followers when their empowered decisions and actions bring trouble. A leader only needs to fail to back up a subordinate once for that person to conclude that all the empowerment talk is just rhetoric. Learning how to think of one's co-responsibility with subordinates for decisions and actions can be a major learning challenge for a leader. In fact, it is not an exaggeration to suggest that the whole key to successful and consistent empowerment may lie in this working through of the way responsibility and accountability are going to work. As I have noted, moreover, it is not the learning of one person but the learning of a system of people that is important.

Empowerment implies an ongoing process of ethical dialogue between empowerer and empoweree. This will be a mutual learning process both of each other's values and perspectives and of the ethical subtleties buried in the issues being discussed.

The above discussion implies something about an empowered environment that should be made explicit: *the more thoroughly empowerment is implemented, the more the belief that a single person—the leader—bears ultimate responsibility needs to be modified.* Just *how* the belief needs to be modified is an evolving matter, but today's flatter, more networked, more team-based organizations are exploring these paradoxes of responsibility and are learning new ways of dealing with them.

I have mentioned the performance pressures that pervade the empowerment process. The leader can be expected to be hyper-aware of the imperatives of getting the job done, usually against tight deadlines and within severe budget constraints. *The learning challenge of performance pressure is how to make it real for the empoweree without stifling—or even panicking—him or her.* Similarly, the empoweree has a corresponding learning process to go through in which greater amounts of performance pressure are borne. Clearly empowerment is a teaching process—a point that applies to many of the learning challenges that have been discussed.

In the midst of these performance pressures, leaders in many organizations are finding that they do not know exactly what the content of empowered behavior needs to be. If they knew, many would just tell people to do it and not bother with empowerment! But in a host of ways, organizations are trying to do things they have never done before. Managers everywhere are talking about "writing the book as we go," "business as unusual," "reinventing ourselves," and so forth. These realities are at the same time the chief reasons for empowerment and its chief dangers and instabilities. *The act of empowerment is fundamentally an act of initiating a learning process on the part of all involved.*

The eleven learning challenges I have discussed in this chapter by no means exhaust the variety of issues that can arise. But these challenges seem to be present whenever a managerial leader undertakes to empower followers. One of the chief arguments for empowerment is that the performance of the unit as a whole will improve when empowerment is consistently and effectively practiced. That, however, is a static way of talking. It is more accurate to say that improvements in the substantive performance of the unit depend on the leader's and followers' ability to meet the learning challenges that empowerment entails.

Conclusion

This chapter has tried to portray the general problem of learning that the modern organization contains and has crystallized the problem in what is called the "learning premise": leadership is not learned; it is learning. From that premise it seems to follow that we need to understand a great deal more about the nature of the learning challenges that managerial leaders face. To illustrate the kinds of conceptual and empirical analysis that are needed, the idea of the learning challenge has been specifically applied to the subject of empowerment.

If the analysis in this chapter is valid, however, a major question remains with far-reaching implications. The question can only be named here, but it really is the main reason that this chapter was written. The question is, *what is involved in empowering leaderly learners to more effectively perceive and grapple with the learning challenges of leadership?* At the present time, leaderly learners in management schools and corporate training programs are, at best, getting only casual and anecdotal exposure to the learning premise and the learning challenges of leadership. Instead, they are simply being put through lectures, discussions, and exercises that an instructor has decided are more or less germane to what leadership seems to be about. There is wide agreement that not very much leadership ability is actually fostered in these kinds of sessions. Perhaps if we can learn how to help would-be leaders to think of themselves as lifelong leaderly learners, they will be better equipped for the leadership challenges of present and future organizations.

7

Adult Education as Paradigm Leadership

My focus in this chapter is on adult education and the kind of leadership it requires of educators. All five of the university business schools in which I have worked have been squarely in the business of adult education for managerial leadership. The way I would like to get into this focus is to say a little more about my own experience with adult learners and share some of the issues I see that make the work you are doing worth doing. It will be twenty-five years ago this coming fall that I took my first teaching job as a new assistant professor at UCLA and began immediately—initially to supplement my income—to teach in UCLA Extension. Right away the income became secondary in importance to the fun I was having in the evening program. In the succeeding six years hardly a semester went by that I did not teach in Extension and participate actively in conferences, institutes, and workshops. In the 1970s I moved to the University of Connecticut where again I was very active in Extension and also taught in the downtown Hartford MBA program. At George Washington University virtually all my teaching has been with adults in the evening since our master's and doctoral programs are strongly oriented toward the part-time adult student. It has also been an interesting experience this last year to

Note: Keynote address to the National Conference on the Adult Learner, University of South Carolina, May 1989.

be director of our doctoral program of 180 students and get a closer look at the programmatic issues of an adult-oriented program (our average student is in his or her mid-thirties). Finally, I should note that I have done extensive training of managers in the workplace in corporations, government agencies, health systems, and voluntary organizations. I would like to take credit for wisely choosing human behavior in organizations as my academic field back in 1960, just when demand for it was starting to boom both as an academic field and for training and consulting, but I can't. I chose the field with no thought at all to demand but rather because I loved it and was fascinated by it.

Seven F's for Adult Education

In my travels in adult education I have had unparalleled professional pleasures and satisfactions. I have learned a lot about the adult learner and about what educational institutions do and do not understand about this person. I have been impressed with how hard these students work, how much *fatigue* they often obviously feel, how we unwittingly cater to the workaholic who is unable to stop accepting responsibility and trying to improve himself or herself.

The student's need for *flexibility* arises constantly—in class scheduling, in deadlines for required work, and in the policies and hours of operation of various support services like the library, the computer center, and the registrar.

The adult learner can experience a great deal of *fragmentation* taking a course here and a course there. It is because the person has other responsibilities, of course, but it is almost amusing to me that in our curriculum planning we give such careful attention to sequencing and interfacing courses, and we worry so much about prerequisites, when the average adult student, because of the attenuated program, will not benefit from all this designing and will in fact find most of it irrelevant or a positive impediment to getting through.

I have been relatively embarrassed over the years about campus *facilities* for adult students. Classrooms often are more reminiscent of eighth grade than anything else. Evening classes start in the rush hour, which makes traffic and parking a chronic problem. Administrative offices close just as the student comes on campus. Restrooms are a mess from the day's use. There are often no convenient places to sit down before class. Food is only available from smiling machines. Telephones are few and far between. Professors are not around for consultation. So catch-as-catch-can is the availability of support facilities for part-time evening students on the five campuses I know well that I long ago concluded that the adult learner is relatively a nonperson in his or her own right in the administrative and philosophical eyes of higher education. Far too often, the real operative assumption, whether conscious or not, is that adult education is simply watered-down full-time, "serious" education, basically a sideline to make a few dollars, and should not be permitted to disturb the core competence and identity of the institution.

There's more. The tuition and *fees* the adult student pays rarely are consciously plowed back into services for this student. Especially as the makeup of the student body changes, the adult student is entitled to ask why more resources are not allocated to the part-time evening program. "Why should my tuition support a campus newspaper that never mentions me, a student union that doesn't offer activities after six, and an intramural athletic program that doesn't reach me?" "Why does my tuition buy me a higher proportion of part-time faculty? No matter how well qualified they are, I can see they are second-class citizens in the institution." I think these are reasonable questions. On many campuses the resource allocation policy is a scandal.

So why don't they complain, an administrator might ask? The answer is easy. They aren't organized. They don't know each other. They only see each other in class and they get no time there to discuss their *feelings* with each other. Furthermore, adult learners quite properly do not see it as their responsibility to formulate a more enlightened resource allocation policy. They feel they are entitled to one and should not have to create it. If they don't get it they tend to keep quiet and become resigned. They come to define their experience at the school as putting up with a bunch of annoyances in exchange for a piece of paper. If we asked adult students how they would feel if their employer provided for them and treated them the way their university does, I suspect we might get an interesting set of reactions. They wouldn't all be negative, but I am sure we would hear some things that would embarrass us.

To conclude this list of things I have learned about adult students, I want to mention *faculty*. The term *faculty,* by the way, appears I think only once in the titles of the ninety-odd papers that were written for this conference. I don't know what that is saying. I do know that one hardly ever hears faculty members discussing adult education and the adult learners as important in their own right. The regular mainstream degree programs in management, for example, tend not to contain any explicit assumptions about adult learners, even though they are probably a clear majority of students. In so-called executive MBAs, there will often be a realization that the students are a "tough audience," but this is usually treated as a constraint rather than an opportunity, and the main concession that is made to this tough audience is to give them more time for class discussion and perhaps more frequent classroom breaks.

It is deeply troubling to me that the average faculty member does not regard adult education and the adult learner as anything special. The reason we call the faculty the *faculty* is that it is the means by which an educational institution does whatever it does. The faculty culture has not singled out adult education as a unique mission, even though many individual faculty members have done this. The faculty culture is even faintly contemptuous of adult education and the adult learner. The official myth is that the school has to engage in adult education mainly to make money and to keep the legislature or the employment market happy. But *real education* lies elsewhere than in adult education, or so goes what I think is still the dominant myth.

A close friend is returning to school this fall to finish her degree in fine arts. She is "forty-something" and is the sort of person any of us would be delighted to have in a class. She knows the faculty of the George Washington Business School pretty well, and I asked her which ones she would enjoy having as a professor and which ones she wouldn't. Her two lists were interesting because the names on both lists were professors she would call her friends. But those she would not want as teachers are louder, more aggressive, and more offhand than most faculty. One she called a "manipulator." Two others seem frequently to drink too much. One is prone to make suggestive remarks to women. One, she said, is too snide and cynical. All are perfectly well qualified academically and I think are regarded as highly productive by their colleagues. But it is their qualities as people she was responding to, viewing them as adults through an adult's eyes. What this little exercise suggests to me is that we need to think of faculty as adult learners too. The exercise suggests that their success as teachers of adults depends on their qualities of character as much as on their academic acumen.

An adult student is perceiving and judging the professors far more deeply and astutely than is a twenty-year-old and I think that on those perceptions and judgments rests the subsequent quality of learning that takes place. Here is yet another research question that could be asked of any school's faculty: "Who among us would *we* like to have as our own professor and why, and what does this tell us about our professional development that we should be emphasizing?" Faculty members tend to equate professional development with scholarly development. In adult education it is far more than that. On my friend's list of professors she would like to have, the outstanding qualities were that she felt they were open-minded (which means they viewed themselves as learners), could be trusted, and respected her and cared about her as a person. These qualities are not so surprising. What is surprising, even shocking, is that the informal faculty culture and the formal faculty reward system place so little emphasis on these qualities, and that so many faculty members do not possess the moral character and the interpersonal competence these qualities denote and therefore have so much learning to do. How can we seriously talk about adult education without assessing faculty quality, considering faculty readiness to work with adult learners, and planning faculty development—for the faculty, as I say, is the means by which the institution finally does whatever it does.

So there's a brief survey of what my experience with adult learners has taught me: fatigue, flexibility, fragmentation, facilities, fees, feelings, and faculty. Seven "F's" to ponder. I think we have a lot to do in each category. Do I give us an "F" for our efforts so far? No, but I am sure that much research and theory in adult education covers much of this ground and doubtless explores further issues that I have not thought of. I am delighted that all this work is going on, and I hope it continues and flowers. However, I would like to suggest that all these new programs and all this research is not the only work that adult educators are doing, not the only role you have to play. I encourage you to continue to do this kind of concrete research and innovation, but I also hope that you will think of yourselves as philosophers of what you are doing, philosophers of higher education as it is increasingly going to be in America and worldwide over the next quarter century or so.

The Paradigm Shift That Is Adult Education

My experience teaches me that adult education is really different from the traditional full-time undergraduate college experience. (I should note in passing that many adults are trying to be full-time undergraduates, even though the majority are going part-time during nonwork hours. Even those going full-time constitute quite a different educational cohort; the points I want to make apply to them too.) *You can't extrapolate from the traditional college model to the adult learner.* That's what the main culture of higher education would like to try to do. You know better than I do all the ways this urge manifests itself. I am sure you agree with me that it is a dangerous assumption to make if we are interested in helping adults have a truly quality experience.

The prevailing paradigm that has developed out of the four-year, full-time undergraduate model dominates, indeed engulfs, our thinking. To the extent that adult education and the nature of the adult learner call this prevailing paradigm into question, we have a couple of choices, if we agree with Thomas Kuhn's (1970) theory of how paradigms develop, operate, and change. One choice is to work intuitively at the adult education mission, dealing case by case with the prevailing model that presumes four-year, full-time adolescents as the learners. We proceed piecemeal, solving problems as they arise, letting the adult education programs and our knowledge of the adult learner accumulate as a body of facts and practices but never confronting the ruling model head-on for its own sake. This is the way most of us proceed most of the time, and properly so. It gets the most done at the program level, and it is frankly the most prudent method.

However, the other choice also has its appeal. It is the more confrontational path of consciously redefining the main business of an institution and trying in every way possible to organize by the principles of a new paradigm that is more consciously attuned to the adult learning process and to the ways in which adult learners would like to be participants in an educational institution. It puts adult educators into the role of *new-paradigm leaders*, whereas the first choice puts us more into the role of what we might call *old-paradigm nibblers!*

Paradigm leaders. We have heard a lot about paradigms and paradigm shifts in recent years—and I happen to be one of those who thinks human society is living through a massive set of paradigm shifts in the twentieth century. Less often, though, have I seen discussions of the characteristics of paradigm leaders, how they act, what they value, what their real motives and purposes are.

I wish to suggest that you make both of my choices—that you continue to work away at the concrete business of improving the quality of educational life of the adult learner, but that in a broader sense you try also to think of yourself as a paradigm leader, that is, one whose programs and ideas symbolize and suggest far deeper and more extensive possibilities for change within your institution, in your academic field, or in the professions and occupations you work with. If thousands of us do not do this, our educational establishment will not be able to adapt to the turbulent changes of the modern world. Our colleges and universities are already at serious risk as to their relevance. Adult education, understood paradigmatically, is a promising vector of evolution back to relevance and societal impact.

Because of the pace of change, life has become full-time education. That is the cardinal fact that, engrossed in the ivory tower where so many of us think full-time education occurs, we educators keep misunderstanding and undervaluing. Life is full-time education. We are all learners, and given the pace of change, we are all perpetually high up on the learning curve.

Possibly we who think about and work with the adult learner are exceptions, for we are exposed daily to how much our adult learners already know, already have experienced, already feel, already know about their own learning process. Their full-time education is going on everywhere, not just in our classrooms. The fact is inescapable, anyway, to anyone who has looked at and thought about it. The truth is, the old paradigm disparages the full-time education that occurs in life. The old paradigm is asleep in the information age.

If we are going to be paradigm leaders as well as practical innovators, what is in store for us? What kinds of experiences are we going to have? What kinds of problems will we run into? High orders of leadership and management skill obviously are called for. Moral toughness, too, coupled with the ability to forgive unenlightened academics their obliviousness and vanity, even while helping them to change. Clearly, highly developed coaching skills are needed when students and faculty alike are not too sure of what they are doing, high up as they are on the learning curve.

Beyond this, perhaps we can return to the theorist of paradigm revolution himself, Thomas Kuhn, for some guidance about what is in store for us. Any paradigm, says Kuhn (1970, pp. 182–187), exists as a "disciplinary matrix" that has four broad elements: first, what Kuhn calls "symbolic generalizations," or what I would call the fundamental understandings that are held of how the phenomena within the paradigm work; second, "metaphysical assumptions," that is, what are taken to be the *real* things the paradigm deals with; third, "values," or what is important, what the priorities are, what the basic purposes and meanings of phenomena are within the paradigm; and fourth, "exemplars," the people and events that are taken as the fullest embodiment of the paradigm.

I would like to discuss within each category what a paradigm leader in adult education working with adult learners might expect to encounter from the old paradigm, in other words, what some of the more likely grounds are on which the battles will be fought and leadership displayed. Maybe all this sounds too grand and heroic, but I hope not. My intent is to build an agenda and forecast a professional future for folks just like us.

Symbolic Generalizations

Symbolic generalizations define how the process is supposed to work. A great deal could be said in this category, for it basically deals with how we conceive of the whole educational process—the things we are sure of about how it should go. The characteristics of the adult learner force change in this category. The more we learn about the adult learner, the more we can reevaluate the efficacy of various tried-and-true processes in education, from the way we handle the admissions process to the way we define and administer final exams. The paradigm shift comes in making education more *learner-centered*. The old four-year, full-time model is not learner-centered.

It originally was faculty-centered, and more recently it is institution-centered; that is, it proceeds according to the institution's needs and priorities.

In developing a learner-centered approach, there is a chance that the four-year, full-time experience will itself be improved. Learner-centered techniques were first invented, principally by NTL in the 1940s and 1950s, not for students but for teachers, that is, adult learners. It was the teacher-trainers who subsequently used them in the classroom with four-year, full-time undergraduates. The learner-centered model must be seen in terms of a paradigm shift, though; it is not just a set of minor modifications. If it is viewed as no big deal, the old paradigm will compromise and undercut a learner-centered philosophy in a hundred different ways.

The classroom process itself is one of the clearest ways in which the learner-centered approach differs from the instructor-centered approach. This is a commonplace. The strategic issue we have not solved is how to foster significant numbers of genuinely learner-centered faculty. Nothing can wreck a learner-centered design faster than having someone at the front of the room who thinks that his or her role is to supply technical content in as rapid-fire a way as possible. That really is the old paradigm par excellence.

Another powerful example of the old paradigm is seen in accreditation criteria. Many of us have run afoul of accreditation criteria, with their specifications of admissions criteria, faculty credentials, class composition, program length, and so forth. Accreditation criteria look backward to best practice from the past. They cannot embody innovation; they cannot authorize what has not been done before. They constitute a monolith of conventionality. I hasten to add that we are not immune ourselves. As we get clearer on programs for adult learners, we will probably evolve accreditation criteria for them. There is something eternally seductive about accreditation, and no program is exempt from the temptation. Get the accreditation standards that apply to any degree program you are designing for adult learners. Those standards will provide you with a very nice road map of the problems you are going to run into as you proceed.

The final symbolic generalization I'd like to mention is grades. They embody sacred truth in the old paradigm. They are not unimportant to the adult learner, but I think they have a very different meaning and probably cannot therefore be designed and administered in the same way. I would like to believe that adult learners are more interested in *adult* feedback on their work. "B+—Nice try" on a term paper that one labored hours and hours over is not what I would call adult feedback. The adult learner is more insightful about and sensitive to the essential arbitrariness of all grading, no matter what the subject is. The adult learner can see just how tenuous and shallow the validity of grades is, how little they actually say about a person. It is not an exaggeration to suggest that the adult learner challenges and perhaps demolishes the sanctity of grades as traditionally conceived—the adult learner, that is, who is viewed through the eyes of a new paradigm. We know that most adults will knuckle under to grades as traditionally administered if they don't get any support for doing otherwise, no matter how idiotic they privately consider the process to be or how disgusted they may become with a professor who uses grades as a cattle prod.

The category of symbolic generalizations asks us to be aware of all the ways we are changing the way the educational process is supposed to work. The more we can see what we are proposing as basic changes in the process, the more we will be aware of our opportunities and responsibilities as paradigm leaders.

Metaphysical Assumptions

The second category of Kuhn's disciplinary matrix is metaphysical assumptions—what is taken by the paradigm to be real. As a professor I am keenly aware of the reality of my academic credentials, for example! What the old paradigm ignores, of course, is that the academic credentials of anyone out of school for ten years or more are fully depreciated! The old paradigm doesn't attach reality to that little detail.

Academic credentials mean something different to the adult learner. There is more interest in what the professor can do now than in what degree she or he once earned. When the finance professor talks about the economy and the stock market to the twenty-year-old, the student takes notes. A student who is thirty-five goes home and calls his or her broker! In many ways the adult learner is *more* interested in the reality of credentials than the adolescent—the current reality. The trouble is, the old paradigm is relatively indifferent to how current the professor is. This means that a new paradigm oriented toward the adult learner has to raise a whole set of questions about instructor qualifications that the old paradigm doesn't want to bother with. In my opinion, we can do no greater service to higher education than to creatively rethink the nature and meaning of instructor qualifications under a learner-centered model of the process.

A second reality that I think the adult learner challenges is the whole area of subject matter. The old paradigm tends to subordinate subject matter to academic bookkeeping. It starts with a calculation based on four years, two semesters or three quarters per year, a "full load" defined as four or five courses, a course defined as a certain number of hours per session and sessions per week, and *then* asks how various subjects can be trimmed and shaped to fit logically within this structure.

No one I know thinks that subject matter is properly or validly packaged this way. Everyone agrees that it does violence in various degrees to the integrity of subject matter. But the agreement is only verbal, and I believe that very little innovation would be going on if it were not for adult learners. They know two things that younger students don't know. The first is that all subject matter looks different out in society and the world of work than it does in the course syllabus and the reserve book room—all subject matter, everything we teach. The second is that all subject matter is *inter-related* and that all divisions of it are arbitrary. The adult learners sitting in class know this, even though they might not know that they know. Awareness will come if we take seriously our opportunities for paradigm leadership.

Sometimes the adult learner is sneered at by old paradigm aristocrats for being excessively preoccupied with the marketability of the course material. I suppose there are adult students who regard the course only as a tool that will earn them money or a promotion. Again, though looked at through a newer paradigm, we see a learner understandably concerned with the meaning of the material to the other sectors of his or her life. We see a learner uncomfortable with being asked to accept on faith alone that the material is relevant— especially when the speaker is a professor about whom the adult learner may have some concerns, as I mentioned previously. There is very little systematic evaluation of the meaning and value of what we teach in higher education. Let's face it: what little we do at all is mainly guesswork. The adult learner wants more than this, and if we take the adult learner seriously we are going to have to change our paradigm.

Space prohibits me from continuing to review the changes in what is treated as real by one paradigm or another. I do know that the real quality of an institution depends very little on the record of its basketball team, the number of acres of grass on the campus, the number of books in the library or Ph.D.'s on the faculty. I know the student's needs are just as real as the faculty's. I know the nonacademic staff's needs are real, something that most colleges and universities would prefer not to consider too carefully because it can be expensive. The more learner-centered and adult-oriented an institution is, the more it will find itself questioning the cherished realities that have accumulated under the old paradigm. The new realities that develop as we seek to work with the adult learner—these too will be discovered in the process of our paradigm leadership.

Values

Kuhn's third element in the matrix that defines a paradigm—values—are matters of the greatest importance. As paradigm shifts occur, things that were previously valued may recede in significance; matters that were not valued, or even more troubling matters that were disvalued and avoided, may assume new prominence and significance. We know the intensity of the debates over values that accompany these shifts. It led one student of paradigm shifts—perhaps it was Kuhn himself—to say that old theories don't die; old *theorists* die. Rarely, in other words, do we fundamentally change our minds. Rather, newer, younger workers adopt the new values as part of their normal approach, and older workers and their values pass from the scene.

Has this been happening with the adult learner in higher education? Are younger faculty and educational administrators more oriented to the adult learner and an adult-oriented educational mission now than, say, twenty years ago? I don't know for sure. That's yet another strategic research question. Here is my hunch, though. My hunch is that mainstream higher education does not value the adult learner much more highly than in the 1970s or 1960s. I can't prove it, but the value of the adult learner just doesn't seem to me to be much more "in the air" now than it was twenty years ago. There are two exceptions to this generalization, one that is possible and one I am sure of. The possible exception is that over the past twenty years certain institutions have energetically and creatively oriented themselves toward the adult learner, have executed the value shifts. Such institutions are the exemplars that are Kuhn's fourth category of paradigm evidence and should be paid attention to.

The exception I am sure of is that other organizations, notably Fortune 500 corporations, have moved aggressively into adult education and now offer a bewildering array of courses and other programs, taught by men and women who could as easily be faculty members in universities—except that they are not. I do not need to persuade you of the extent of this trend. I do note, though, that most of the writers and researchers in this area are academically based. Ten years from now, I think it likely that corporate presenters will substantially outnumber academics at a conference such as this one.

Why would corporations move into leadership in adult education? Partly to meet their own needs, but partly because there are a couple of billion *adults* in the Third World who would like a college degree. That, folks, is what businesspeople call a market! And that is in addition to the seventy-five million or more Americans who are serious adult learners today, whether they are actually registered for anything or not.

If there is anything to this concern of mine about whether higher education values the adult learner as more than a source of revenue, I hope the question will occupy a good deal of attention at this conference. If you can say that your efforts are understood and appreciated by the key people on your campus and the adult learner is viewed as a key client, then there is no problem. But if your sense is of something less than that, you are again thrust into the role of paradigm leader.

Exemplars

The final category of Kuhn's matric is *exemplars*: people, events, and physical symbols that embody the whole approach the paradigm is concerned with. Exemplars can be pointed to, discussed, and debated. They show the paradigm concretely as a whole, for the paradigm does not describe a list of attributes or a piecemeal collection but an integrated, whole approach.

In various ways in this chapter I have been trying to challenge us concerning the true dimensions of programs for the adult learner.

They shouldn't be such hard learners to serve—they're adults, after all, and they want to learn. The thing that makes educational programming for them hard is that we have this hypnotic four-year, full-time model to contend with. No one other than someone who is constrained by it is going to change it. My sense is that those of us interested in the adult learner are such people. Let's get on with the leadership the change requires.

8

Seven Process Frontiers for Organization Development

Here's a new definition of organization development (OD), to replace the dozens that have been offered over the years. Like any good definition, it says a lot to those who already know what OD is and communicates practically nothing to those who don't. But here it is at the outset, because a basic thesis of this chapter is that OD is in danger of forgetting this definition and, if it does, it will become defunct as a profession and an organizational function. The definition is this:

> Organization development is an organizational process for understanding and improving any and all substantive processes an organization may evolve for performing any tasks and pursuing any objectives.

Exploring a Process Definition of OD

A process for improving processes—that's what OD has basically been about for the last twenty-five years or so. This definition helps us to understand why it is so hard to explain what OD is: without

---

Note: Originally published as a chapter in W. Sikes, A. Drexler, and J. Gant (eds.), *The Emerging Practice of Organization Development.* Alexandria, Va.: NTL Institute, 1989. Reprinted, slightly edited, with permission.

the substantive organizational processes in view, whether they consist of planning, group meetings, superior-subordinate communications, or whatever, it is virtually impossible to say what OD is going to contribute. One has to know quite a bit about these substantive processes and quite a bit about the various ways that they can become confused, blocked, or otherwise screwed up, in order to imagine that there might be a type of professional who specializes in helping to sort out how the processes are supposed to work, why they aren't working, and what might be done about it.

The definition also helps us to understand why OD has always been such a miscellaneous collection of loosely related concepts, theories, research findings, and techniques (sometimes bordering on "gimmicks"). If it is going to be relevant to and responsive to the full range of processes one might find in the modern organization, it freezes itself into one theory or doctrine at its peril. Therefore, OD has been and continues to be existentially unable to say exactly what it is about. OD is basically a process of continual learning.

The definition clarifies another of OD's most frustrating features: its unwillingness to take a stand and declare how it thinks things ought to be or, rather, particular consultants' unwillingness in relation to particular clients. OD writers *have* written eloquently and movingly about how organizations ought to be, but in relation to particular organizational projects, your friendly OD consultant has usually been rather hesitant to declare positively how things ought to be. Unfortunately, the result has been to give terms like "facilitator" and "process consultant" a connotation of wishy-washiness, indecisiveness, even lack of moral courage. The new definition makes it clear, however, that OD's interest is in the substantive process and what it needs in order to work better. The consultant usually does not want to take the responsibility for prescribing ways to fix the process, because this usually involves technical expertise that the consultant does not have. OD's assumption has been, I think, that almost any organizational process will work if the people involved in it want to make it work; the *problem* lies in the way people are working with each other around the process in question, and that is what the OD person would like to help with. (Where a substantive process is indeed so flawed that even the best-intentioned and most effectively organized people still can't make it work, OD's assumption has been that these people are perfectly competent to detect these flaws themselves and figure out what substantive changes ought to be made, but that they may need some help in getting together in their perception of the flaws and talking through what to do about them. This would be where OD would try to help.)

These have not been merely the abstract questions and criticisms that can be made of a profession that calls itself a process for improving processes. They can be tough, confronting, even destructive attacks, launched by people in the organization who consider themselves perfectly competent to conduct its processes with no outside facilitation needed. OD people have put up with a lot of sarcasm, have been the butt of many jokes, have had cause many times to doubt themselves and their motives, and have been tempted to dive in and play the same power games that everyone else is playing—the very power games that are fouling up the organization's rational processes for doing what it says it is in business to do.

In the face of this pressure to justify itself, "pay its way," and so forth, OD has developed extraordinary expertise in helping with a few organizational processes. But sadly, it has sometimes drifted away from its expertise as a process for helping with process. The remainder of this chapter will discuss a few of the processes OD has become very competent about, identify a few of the departures from its historic competence, and discuss briefly seven organizational processes that are deeply in need of the kind of assistance OD can render.

OD's Process Accomplishments

Any declaration of what OD's primary achievements have been is guaranteed to be controversial. But here, anyway, are my candidates. As a generalization, OD has become very competent at helping with any organizational processes that have to do with (1) power sharing or (2) lateral communication, especially when they are occurring around a table in some team or committee meeting.

Under the heading of *power sharing* I include all the work OD has done to help managers become more participative, more open to feedback and disagreement, more interested in the points of view of those down the line in the organization. This includes the work OD has done to help managers change their attitudes about their people and to help lower-level workers see the higher-ups differently. This interest in and skill with the process of power sharing probably derives from the enormous influence on OD of Douglas McGregor's (1960) work, coupled with research done all through the 1940s, 1950s, and into the 1960s on democratic versus authoritarian leadership.

It is important to note that OD's work on power sharing has not been matched by equal interest in or skill with the process of concentrating power in the offices of supervisors, managers, and leaders. OD has tended to call these processes "politics" and "power games" and has not tried very often to help with them. There are quite legitimate situations in today's turbulent organizations where the establishment and clarification of power are as important as or more important than power sharing. This is not one of the seven "frontiers" I discuss later in this chapter, but it can be a matter of some significance.

The other major area of expertise OD has developed is in *lateral communication*, helping people to talk to each other when they are relative equals and they have to work together in order to accomplish some task or reach some goal. This is the classic committee meeting situation: the task force, the project group, the "interagency study group," and so forth. It also includes the millions of group meetings that arise in more ad hoc situations such as participation in a voluntary organization or family decision making, and when people are temporarily thrown together for one reason or another. OD knows how to help people work well with each other under these conditions; it is the essence of what has traditionally been called *process consultation*. At its heart is the ability to listen to the way the group is working and not just to the content of what is being said. For all the increase in awareness of the so-called group process issues that have gradually permeated the culture, it is still true that in the heat of the moment, people's understanding of the importance of process often deserts them precisely at the moment when it is needed most; therefore, there will always be a need for process consultants—at least as long as humans continue to be beings whose feelings sometimes lead them to say and do things to others that in a calmer moment they might not do.

Analogous to McGregor's influence on power sharing, the roots of OD's skill in facilitating lateral relationships probably lie in T-groups and individual therapy, where the *meaning* of what a person says, and not just its manifest content, is the primary thing to be understood. OD is very good at helping people to understand others' meanings because of this long experience with groups whose whole purpose is to help people understand themselves and each other.

In addition to power sharing and the facilitation of lateral communication, OD has been developing expertise with a few other organizational processes. Career planning and development is one. Stress management is another. Facilitation of communication across the deep gulfs of gender, racial, and ethnic differences would be a third, although I also will treat this as one of the seven frontiers I discuss later in the chapter. In addition to such relatively well-established areas of professional practice (and you are invited to think of others), there are also dozens of specific fields with which one OD consultant or another has developed expertise. Helping organizations to shrink themselves in as honest and healthy a way as possible is one example. Helping organizations to merge with each other is another. Helping organizations think through executive search processes is a third from among many possible specific applications.

The point I am making is that there are a relatively few organizational processes that virtually all OD people understand pretty

well and can routinely help organizations with. A few other organizational processes exist that we might say the profession has been
edging into. And then there are a huge number that aren't seen as
the core of the profession but that a few consultants have become
very adept at using.

Problems with OD

The seven frontiers mentioned in this chapter's title are intended
to expand the core of what the mainstream OD profession is in
modern organizations. Before I proceed to discuss these seven frontiers, though, I want to say a few things about where I think OD has
been going wrong in the last ten years or so.

In a word, I think OD has been losing its process focus. This is
the dark side of its response to all the pressure and criticism it has
received from hard-nosed, bottom-line-oriented managers. The
bright side is that it has become *very* adept at helping with a few
kinds of organizational processes. However, in not understanding
the definition of itself I gave at the outset of this chapter, OD has
been drifting over into substantive areas, and more and more OD
professionals have been turning themselves into experts on leading-
edge issues in human resources management and development.
Make no mistake, we desperately need experts on leading-edge
issues in human resources management, especially since it appears
that line managers are finally coming to realize that all their plans
for the future hinge on having more or less the right people in the
right places at the right times who are more or less selected, trained,
and rewarded in the right ways, with systems in place that more or
less provide the employee assistance that is needed to those who for
one reason or another are having trouble coping with life in the
organization. I say "more or less" repeatedly here because none of
this is or ever will be an engineering science of any precision.

None of this expertise, however, is what OD has been historically. It is not what OD is by the definition I gave. And it will not

replace the need for "a process for improving processes" in the future. The more organizations try to do, the more flexible they try to stay, the more carefully they allocate their resources, the wider the variety of people they try to employ—the more, in general, they try to remain internally coherent *and* externally adaptive to the turbulent world around them—the more they are going to need a profession whose expertise is in conducting itself as an "organizational process for understanding and improving any and all substantive processes an organization may evolve for performing any tasks and pursuing any objectives."

With so many OD professionals coming to specialize in one or two particular kinds of substantive processes, the danger is that the general process skills they employ in this work will become lost to view. Process skills are terribly ethereal things in the best case; we just barely are able to say what they are in team development or in helping superiors to share power with subordinates. When the process skills are being employed in more remote substantive areas, such as facilitating the installation of a computer-based management information system (where "remote" means an issue not generally understood in much detail by the OD profession), it is highly likely that what the consultant is actually doing to help the installation process along is utterly invisible to the rest of the profession, to line management, and, worst of all, to newcomers in the profession. This type of invisible exercise of process skills is becoming more and more common in OD. The settings in which people are exercising their process skills are becoming more and more various and disparate, with the result that it is harder and harder to sustain the generic view of the profession that our definition declares.

Concomitant with the invisible exercise of process skills is another trend that actually accelerates and intensifies the loss of our generic definition. This is the tendency of these consultants, when they do try to communicate what they do to their colleagues and the outside world, to talk about the substance of their contribution to the situation. By "substance," I mean the theory they may be teaching their clients, the instruments they use for collecting data on the client system, the way they array these data in tables and graphs, the design they employ for workshops they conduct for their clients, and, if all this weren't enough, the aspirations they have for further collecting their consulting expertise into sets of things they can leave with the client, do for the client, indeed, *sell to* the client. This is the dark side: it is so hard to explain to a client what a process consultant does; it's easier to say, "Read this book," "Go through this exercise," "Watch this videotape," than it is to say, "I'm going to charge you cash money for sitting with you and helping you think through how you've been doing, what you want to do next, and how you might go about doing it."

Clients, of course, themselves under pressure to show "deliverables" from the internal or external OD consultant they use, don't want to hear the "I'm going to sit with you . . ." message either. They want to show the vice president for human resources the terrific workbook their OD consultant is disseminating throughout the organization.

Process skills are as important as ever, but when OD consultants get together to talk shop these days, they talk more and more about copyrights, marketing strategies, and the prospects for computerizing a questionnaire and less and less about the sheer process of working with a particular client and how they are feeling about it.

I alternate in my feelings about all this between sadness and amusement. The sadness comes from the realization that we're going to have to invent process skills all over again; we can't get along without them. Terrible things are going to continue to happen in organizations whose substantive processes are out of control and inaccessible to intervention (the IRS computer debacle? the space shuttle explosion? Exxon's two-billion-dollar bath in office systems?). The amusement comes from the realization that the way OD is going these days, all the systems and instrumentations and behavioral objectives OD consultants are merchandising are themselves going to require lots of old-style process facilitation to have any hope of accomplishing in organizations what they promise. I wonder how many OD consulting groups have faced up yet to how much they need an OD consultant to help them connect all this technology to their client organization.

The Seven Frontiers

The core of OD, I have been arguing, does not lie in the content of organizational operations—what I have been calling substantive processes. Nor does it lie, in my opinion, in the proliferation of ideas and techniques and paraphernalia that ostensibly are things that OD can "do" for its clients. The core of OD—what it can do for its clients that no one else can do—lies in its ability to help its clients design, implement, evaluate, and improve the substantive processes the client needs to operate in order to fulfill its mission and be the kind of organization it wants to be. OD's competence is in developing processes that help with processes.

This way of thinking about OD requires OD to keep up with the kinds of operational processes that organizations are evolving. But because OD tends not to think of itself *clearly* as being in the business of evolving processes to help with processes, we have a situation today in which organizations increasingly are having problems OD hardly knows exist. In addition, OD possesses few intervention processes for being helpful in these areas. In the remainder of this chapter, I briefly discuss seven new operational processes that are acutely in need of OD assistance. In saying that OD seems to be unaware of these frontiers, I fully recognize and applaud the individual OD professionals who are working in their own ways on these kinds of problems. What I am calling attention to is an absence of awareness within the profession of what is going on and what is at stake. I know that many leading-edge consultants themselves wonder whether anyone else in the profession cares about the kind of work that needs to be done in modern organizations.

The seven frontiers where new facilitative processes are needed are as follows:

1. The process of finding, developing, understanding, and evaluating relatively high-level managers and leaders, including the processes by which they work with each other on behalf of the organization. Call this *top-management development* as a generic process.

2. The process of understanding ongoing and sometimes very rapid changes in the basic nature of the organization's main business or area of activity. Call this the *what business are we in?* process.

3. The process of discovering, evaluating, installing, and operating new technologies of all kinds for both the core mission and all support functions. Call this the *digesting new technology* process.

4. The process whereby all the new expertise in human resources planning, management, and development comes to be understood and effectively utilized by the organization. Call this the process of *integrating new ideas about human resources*.

5. The processes whereby organization members try to understand the basic nature of their organization, with its opportunities and problems in the world it lives in. Call these *sophisticated diagnostic processes* for lack of a better generic phrase.

6. The processes organizations are beginning to experiment with in response to the continuous turbulence that they live in. Call these *permanent white water strategies*.

7. The gradually dawning awareness in organizations that morals and ethics are involved in everything that happens, whether they are discussed and debated or not. I think that this set of trends can appropriately be called *the manager as a moral agent*.

Remember that these seven frontiers are *not* OD processes. They are categories within which organizations are trying to do new and different things. They are categories in which organizations need help. I am suggesting that they are categories toward which OD could fruitfully direct its facilitative skills in the future. (It should be emphasized that these categories are by no means exhaustive. They cover a lot of ground, but hardly the whole territory of the postindustrial age.)

Top-Management Development

Perhaps the most complete way to make this point is to note that everything top managers do in organizations is organizational behavior. From the very beginning, OD has concerned itself with organizational behavior, yet it has not had a great deal of influence on how top managers are chosen, what they do, or how they work together. The process we are talking about is the general process of the governance and guidance of the organization as a whole. OD has not had much impact on this level of operations partly because OD people have not understood what the needs are; partly because, like everyone else, OD people are a little awed by people of high power and authority; and partly because people of high power and authority are constrained both by their roles and by their own self-concepts from asking for the help they know they need.

However, the situation is changing. More and more studies are coming out about what top managers are like and about what they do, some written by top managers themselves. Fortune 500 companies are finally facing up to the need to consciously develop more men and women who are qualified for positions of broad responsibility and leadership. The people who are getting into these positions are more and more aware of their own need for continued development and, under the right conditions, are much more approachable than their counterparts were a generation ago.

All of this means that an opportunity is developing for OD to help these men and women be more effective. We speak glibly of the "loneliness of command," but for too long we have not drawn the obvious conclusion: loneliness is an acutely felt need; as an unmet need it can produce enormous amounts of personal stress and distortion of the leadership and decision-making process. It is not just a cliché; it is an opportunity, even a responsibility.

What Business Are We In?

For about twenty-five years, this has been the classic question put to MBAs in capstone courses and executives in strategic-planning seminars. OD is almost totally unaware of it, almost totally unaware that changing technology, economic realities, the global competitive situation, and changing consumer tastes have confronted company after company with this question. Furthermore, it is not just a for-profit corporate question; it faces voluntary organizations, government agencies, education and health systems—everyone. For everyone, the basic reason for existing and the basic terms of success are changing beyond the capacity of traditional definitions of the mission to contain them.

But what pain and confusion and acrimony the asking of this question produces! To paraphrase Dostoyevsky, "If the old mission is dead, then everything is allowed!" This is not too far from the feeling that sweeps through organizations that are struggling with defining themselves for the present and the future. It is not a personal anarchy, for each person feels that he or she understands what the new needs are. But collectively the effect can be anarchic, as one version of what the basic thrust should be vies with another. We open the newspapers daily to read that one faction or another in some large organization has "won out" in a struggle over the basic mission. But as OD people we can at least ask: *must* the articulation of basic new directions be a power-based political process? Are we willing to assume that an essentially Darwinian process is the only one we have when it comes to the determination of basic directions? Is the process of deciding what business we are in inevitably a matter of power politics?

Well, we know two things: we know that power politics need not be the only way that human beings sort out their differences and we know that large organizations are capable of making some very large mistakes that result in very high social and economic costs. No, OD has never acquiesced to the claim that Realpolitik is all there is, and it need not in this case. But how we intervene—how we act in ways that are helpful—is unexplored territory.

Digesting New Technology

Classically, in manufacturing, several different kinds of engineering had to be done in order for some product to be produced at required levels of output and quality and within required cost limits. These included product development engineering, manufacturing engineering, industrial engineering, and more recently quality and value engineering. Systems engineering has attempted to integrate these various perspectives, which all do have to be integrated in order for objectives to be met.

OD has never been very interested in the way an organization tries to adopt and absorb new technology through these various kinds of engineering plus others. In fact, if anything, the engineers who produce the rationalized designs and implementation processes have been the "bad guys" in OD's eyes. Historically there has been some justification for OD's distaste for rationalized designs, for they have contained some very unrealistic and even inhumane assumptions and requirements for the people who operate the engineers' systems.

For two reasons, however, this situation has changed quite markedly in the past decade. First, the technologists are increasingly willing to consider the human implications of their systems. Human factors is an old and well-developed field, of course, but until recently it has tended to restrict itself to the physiological aspects of humans. Now, however, it is rapidly becoming not merely nice but necessary to consider the psychological and interpersonal dimensions. The rapid rise of the field of ergonomics testifies to this renewed interest. OD people may discover that some of these formerly "cold and inhumane" technologists know more about the whole employee than OD does!

Second, the sheer speed of technological change, and its extension into all corners of organizational operations, means that the formerly well-structured systems engineering approach is itself not able to keep up with the pace of change. The systems engineers need help in talking to each other as well as to their users. Nowhere is this situation more apparent than in the hardware and software engineering of computer systems. The power and promise of the technology is not matched by the ability of organizations to comprehend it. We all know brilliant "computer types," for they have been emerging in droves from our universities and the military. But we know far fewer—we may have trouble thinking of any—*social* systems that are managing all this expertise relatively smoothly on behalf of the organization's mission. The brilliant computer types tend to know how to work with others who have their own degree of sophistication in the same sector of the industry they are in. Their capacity to communicate and work productively with others tails off rapidly, however, as they encounter people with kinds and degrees of expertise that are foreign to their own. They need a *lot* of help.

Specifically, it would not be an exaggeration to say that we need virtually a new subprofession of people with OD process skills who are adept at keeping various elements of the overall computer industry in communication with each other, especially since what they do is affecting a relatively nontechnical "user" who today alternates between mystification and fury over the impact of it all.

Integrating New Ideas About Human Resources

As noted earlier in this chapter, it is wonderful that line management seems finally to be realizing that the state of the human resources of an organization is *the* determining factor in the organization's capacity to survive and develop. We need not debate this. But it is also important to note that much of the new human resources expertise we are making available to the organization is "new technology" of just the esoteric sort that was discussed in the previous section. When line management asks for a new reward system, or a series of gender-awareness workshops, or a study of worker attitudes in the organization, it may not realize just how much professional expertise it is turning loose. But it is a great deal, and it promises to continue to increase.

An OD mentality might ask, "Do we really want to take the holistic comprehension of the employee away from the line manager? Do we really want to contribute to a situation where the human resources staff are the only ones who have the behavioral science knowledge?" An OD mentality might begin to wonder how, through some kind of intervention, we can avoid dehumanizing the workforce by recasting it in the abstract categories of modern human resources management. "High Pot" is such a category. In at least four major companies, I have seen the search for young managers of high potential turn into a quasi-scientific testing and assessment program with a quasi-scientifically selected cadre emerging who are then put through a carefully designed series of experiences designed to capitalize on this presumed high potential. In none of the four situations I have seen was anyone managing the relations of the High Pots to each other, to others in the organization, or indeed to themselves and their own awareness of who they were as people. High Pots are a category, and quite likely they are a time line on some human resource planner's annual report of numbers of employees "trained."

"Competency-based management development" is another such category, as is "organizational behavior modification." The point is that with no one paying much attention to these substantive processes of human resources management, we risk leaving management as cut off as ever from its people. Management used to be cut off because of its own Theory X assumptions and suspicions. Now, if the human resources field keeps developing as it has been, management will be cut off because its workforce has been turned into something it can't recognize. To repeat the point I have already made several times: we need more thorough and professional attention to the human resources management issues that exist in organizations. But we *also* need OD process facilitation to help balance this work with all the other things that are going on in the organization.

Sophisticated Diagnostic Processes

Everyone is complaining these days about the highly analytical and impersonal style that young MBAs are learning in our nation's business schools. However, even if there is a withdrawal from the extremely technical analytical approaches that have been employed recently, it is still safe to say that management will remain a far more analytical and quasi-scientific enterprise than it was when OD was first getting started. Cognitive styles have changed permanently, it seems, toward greater presumed rationality in organizational life. This is especially true with the subject of problem identification.

When today's staffer comes through the door and says, "Boss, we've got a problem," it is a certainty that the evidence will not be rumor, hunch, or intuition. The evidence will be data, usually quantitative data. There may well be an analytical model in the background, and if the data are computer-generated, a consciously constructed model will definitely be involved. Human beings in everyday life also operate from models and frames and abstractions. However, the processes by which we develop our everyday models are vastly different from the processes by which analytical models are developed, tested, refined, and utilized. OD's process skills were developed in order to help human beings with different "models" of situations to communicate better with each other, increase their mutual understanding, and thus increase their work effectiveness. OD knows very little about the process skills that are needed when the competing definitions of reality are consciously developed analytical models that purport to be devoid of the distortions that result from human quirks and idiosyncrasies.

This problem is manifesting itself all over the organizational world. In the form it usually takes, someone with up-close, hands-on familiarity with some issue or process is astonished to discover what the modelers have made out of it for purposes of computer simulations and analyses. One example that is gaining prominence very quickly is the subject of organizational culture. Almost by definition, everyone understands the culture that she or he lives in, whether it is an organizational, ethnic, national, racial, or professional culture. There now exist, however, culture "maps" and "profiles" and other diagnostic devices that bypass the intuitive familiarity of members in favor of standardized categories of cultural "factors." The intent is to teach managers about culture so that they presumably will have more control over it and the ability to change it if they want to. What I wish to call attention to here is the speed with which the subject of culture is being converted into a highly rationalized set of categories that is taught to management as *the* way to think about culture. There will be competing models, however, so some process skills will need to be exercised to help management figure out what it all means.

We have already been through this process with dozens of organizational subjects, of which strategic planning and excellence are two that I am personally very familiar with. The process skills that are needed are a combination of traditional help on the interpersonal dimension and the new ingredient of help with the basic thinking processes that are now more and more important. The process skills of the future are going to involve a lot more skill with logic, with data, with what science is and isn't and can and can't do, and with how all of this interweaves in interpersonal communication with all the other psychological factors that are involved. In brief, we are moving rapidly into modes of new language systems and forms of consciousness for which old-style process skills are simply inadequate.

Permanent White Water Strategies

"We tend to assume that we paddle our organizational canoes on calm, still lakes, and that periodically we have to go through some temporary white water to get to the next stage," a conference participant observed recently. "But it seems to me," he continued, "that we never get out of the white water. We think things will settle down after whatever is now upsetting things is over, but things never settle down because some other upset always comes along to keep things churned up."

Many years ago, Kurt Lewin created a simple but vivid model of the change process, a model that has appeared in various guises in OD thinking ever since: *unfreezing-moving-refreezing*. Even our most contemporary thinkers on such topics as transitions and organizational transformation still seem to make the assumption that things will settle down again after the changes being proposed are implemented. I think one can detect a growing awareness of and interest in the permanent white water condition, though. "Flexibility" is one of the key strategic objectives of most organizations these days. We have been speaking of the environment as "turbulent" for years. "Light and agile" is the phrase CEO John Welch of General Electric Company likes to use to describe what he wants for the company. The phrase "the fast track," for all the questions we can raise about its superficiality, nevertheless signals a desire to keep moving and not become entangled in intractable problems. Second and third careers are now things people plan for, rather than things they are shocked and upended by.

Coming to terms with the existential fluidity and uncertainty that has evolved in our culture calls for a very high order of process skills. OD has not been indifferent to this area, but most of its work has been directed to the personal level to help individuals cope with the stresses and transitions in their lives. The need at the institutional level is acute too, however. OD is doing much less at this level and seems not to even understand what the issues are. But consider the process skills that might be needed in helping an organization of the size and with the traditions of a General Electric become more light and agile. If this is not to be done with a meat ax, some very thoughtful facilitating needs to go on.

This problem of permanent white water is obviously quite strongly influenced by the other issues discussed on this list. I include it as a separate item, however, because unless it is addressed directly we may think that the other six problems are merely problems of "unfreezing-moving-refreezing."

The Manager as a Moral Agent

In mainstream management textbooks, one does not find managers and leaders discussed as moral agents, that is, as individuals who, by their actions and inactions, strongly influence the moral quality of the whole organization. Of course, one doesn't find managers and leaders treated as amoral either. Rather, the assumption is that for all practical purposes the moral question is settled: the pursuit of the organization's objectives within the boundaries of the law is the primary moral standard. This is an instrumental morality where the more effectively and efficiently someone can pursue objectives, the more moral she or he is. This way of thinking traces back through John Dewey to William James and the pragmatists. Chester Barnard was one of the first to thoroughly articulate it as an ethical standard on which managers could rely.

Not surprisingly, OD has only concerned itself with morals and ethics when it has felt that its client-managers were behaving unethically by its own standards. OD set its morals and ethics *against* management's, in other words, when such confrontation was needed. Interestingly, so have virtually all other technical and staff specialties we find in the organization, and so have all external constituencies of organizations. Just like OD, when they thought management was acting wrongly by their own standards of what was right and wrong, they did not hesitate to speak up. The result of this cacophony of conflicting moral judgment is that management has been put in an essentially impossible position. Managers feel that they are supposed to be all things to all people. They say, "You can't please everybody." "You can't win, you can't break even, you can't even get out of the game," goes an aphorism of great appeal to practicing managers.

Each of us, in other words, sees the manager as a moral agent, and so do managers themselves, for they too want to be able to feel they are doing the right thing by their own standards. It is not surprising that in the last ten or fifteen years, this mythical bottom line has become so important to managers. It is easier to understand why they cling to it so desperately if we think of it as a moral standard rather than an accountant's category.

Managers are moral agents because they try to do the right thing themselves and because everyone around them evaluates their actions in moral terms. But the result of all the cross-cutting evaluation is conflict, misunderstanding, and resentment as often as it is mutual respect and commitment. *Someone* needs to help members and constituents of organization sort out their values, their morals, and their standards. What is needed are process skills as practiced by someone like an OD consultant, but it has to be someone whose own highest value is in helping others come together on their values. It is not a role OD has been playing very energetically; however, it is a role that is desperately needed if organizations and their managers are to avoid paralysis.

Conclusion

I have named and discussed seven broad areas of organizational operations where, I have argued, process facilitation of the sort OD has traditionally practiced is badly needed. But I have also engaged in a bit of criticism of the OD profession and its apparent inability to bring its traditional process skills to bear on these issues.

It is worth repeating one more time that the kinds of process skills OD uniquely possesses lie in helping other organizational processes to go more smoothly and effectively. This, we have proposed, has always been OD's unique competence, whether it understood itself this way or not. If anything, as organizations and life become more disconnected and problematic, the process skills that help substantive processes happen are more needed than ever. Is there anyone else around besides the OD profession with the competence and the will to deliver them?

Part IV

Spirit

9

The Inherent Spirituality
of Organizations

The public view of formal work organizations, both academically and popularly, has tended to be that organizations possess a fixed character, defined by such variables as their mission, size, technology, structure, and operating environment. This is not to say that there is no such thing as organizational *dynamics*, but rather that these dynamics have been presumed to operate homeostatically. While we do talk about various kinds of fundamental metamorphoses—"transformation" is a currently popular word—most theorists nonetheless treat organizations as having enough continuing, identifiable coherence to warrant talking about them as if they were real entities, not imaginary concepts.

Although certain religious and other idealistically oriented organizations have considered their character to be defined "under God," the preponderance of formal organizations are seen, both subjectively and objectively, as purely secular. Further, within the mainstream of organization and management theory and practice, the tendency has been to treat a divine foundation as a datum of organizational behavior, that is, something members may believe, which thus influences their behavior toward each other and their

---

Note: An earlier version of this chapter was presented at the Academy of Management national meetings, Miami Beach, Fla., August 1991, as part of a symposium titled "Organizations as Spiritual Settings: Implications for Organization Theory and Organizational Change and Development."

environment but which is neither true nor untrue from the stand-point of the investigator. Can there be a divinely grounded organi-zational behavior—that is, a serious study in which organizational events are assumed to be codetermined by human and divine action? A definitive answer to this question is not known, but the assumption of this chapter is that little if any work within main-stream theory and research has included a divine grounding as part of the data to be understood. Even investigators who privately may believe thoroughly in the divine grounding and guidance of orga-nizations tend to leave such beliefs tacit when studying empirical organizational behavior. We can note the Pilgrims praying for the *Mayflower* to complete its voyage safely, for example, but as inves-tigators we have only asked about the material function of such behavior, not about its truth.

This relative absence of attention to the implications of spiri-tual foundation has not prevented various organization members from privately perceiving their organizations in spiritual terms. The perceptions can run from godliness to godlessness. Some members believe absolutely in a divine cognizance of the organization and perhaps in divine intervention; others are just as sure that the orga-nization is a purely secular phenomenon. One assumption of this chapter is that organization members are not morally and spiritu-ally indifferent to the character of the organizations that populate their lives, just as they are not indifferent to any other influences on the perceived meaning of their lives; they will tend to have some position that is relatively available to consciousness.

The view of organizations taken in this chapter is the social con-structionist view that organizations have no objective character apart from the system of perceptions of the individuals and groups who comprise them and/or are their stakeholders, including observers. These perceptions can be extraordinarily stable, widely held, and self-reinforcing, thus making it easy to think that they are objective and "given." But they are not. Instead, in Weick's phrase, they must be continually reaccomplished (Weick, 1969, p. 36). If there is inherent spirituality in organizations, it is to be found in the experiences members and others have in them. This chapter explores the possibility that events in organizations and their environments are increasing members' need to find spiritual meaning in their organizations.

The Changing Meanings of "Being Organized"

A major hypothesis of this chapter is that we are living in a period (and indeed have been for several decades) when new reaccomplishments are emerging and gathering force. The organization is coming to mean something different than it has in the past. We are asking that organizations pay more attention to their customers, that they value quality production and service much more highly, that they act affirmatively to increase their demographic diversity, that they empower lower-level people, and that leaders be filled with vision. We are asking that organizations think and act globally and that they change themselves into continuous learning systems. They are being asked more and more to incorporate systems of artificial intelligence as virtual members. We are asking organizations to structure themselves in networks rather than in hierarchies, and we are asking that they become vastly more flexible and agile in their conduct. These and many other kinds of changes both express the new meanings we are projecting onto our sense of being organized and capture the crisis of meaning that is widely felt by those who are seeking these redefinitions.

It seems unlikely that a new paradigm of what it means to be organized will emerge in as clear-cut and credible a form as Weberian bureaucracy and its permutations have been. It seems more likely that for the foreseeable future, we will be continuing to probe and experiment with what it means to be organized, and that a major component of the paradigm itself will be to avoid fixed, monolithic definitions of what an organization is. In current literature we have giants and elephants learning to dance, and we have flexibility and agility as watchwords. We have Tom Peters declaring, albeit in his distinctly undancelike way, that the name of the game is "flat, fluid, and get on with it" and that "speed is life." It seems likely, therefore, that we will not *feel* as organized as it might have been possible to feel a generation ago, although the process of letting go of that need and feeling will doubtless be a painful one. The way so-called matrix structures tend to remain as frustrating, ill-defined, and unstable organizing processes nearly thirty years after their invention is evidence that feeling organized in the future is not going to be what it has been in the past.

The Grounds of Coherence and Meaning

To say that there is a "feeling of being organized" is to say that organization members are able to find credibility and meaning in their organizational surroundings. This does not require that they like the policies and processes around them, only that these ongoing organizational events be meaningful for them. The feeling of being organized is nothing less than a sense that the organizational patterns one is living with possess coherence and meaning. The question then arises of what the new grounds of coherence and meaning will be. How will organization members and stakeholders maintain a sense of meaningfulness in the midst of these substantially changed operating conditions?

In the past, the feeling of coherence in organizations have resided in the stable, reliable personalities of leaders, and in traditions of strong commitment to quality, to employees, and/or to customers. Some organizations have been filled with missionary zeal for what they do, even if it is fairly humble and mundane. An actual nobility ("high meaning") exists in an organization that has succeeded in performing its mission at a high level of excellence over a long period of time. Less glamourous but no less powerful is the meaning many organizations have achieved in the past through being absolutely secure places of employment, thus fostering extraordinary loyalty in members. Indeed, it may not be an exaggeration to say that security of employment, prior to about the mid-1970s, was the chief means by which organizations established themselves in members' minds as meaningful and valuable.

More recently we have seen organizations achieve a sense of coherence by an all-out commitment to win, be number one, be world-class. The rapid rise of interest in the total quality criteria of the Malcolm Baldrige National Quality Award is evidence of this. We are currently in a period where the assumption is that an almost maniacal commitment to the mission, with special attention to the customer, is the way that organizations are going to create and sustain meaning in the eyes of members and stakeholders, and no actions by leaders to achieve this degree of commitment are seen as too extreme. Undoubtedly, Western organizations can benefit from increased clarity, consensus, and commitment to the mission. However, there is more than a whiff of totalitarian fervor in the way organizations are currently being trumpeted as settings for all-out, unremitting, unequivocal commitment to the mission. This degree of iron unanimity may work against the kind of flexibility and agility that organizations need in order to navigate in the permanent white water of the modern environment.

Stresses on Contemporary Groundings

Despite all of this effort to create meaning for organization members and stakeholders, the fixity of product qualities is gone, as is the nobility of traditional organizational missions. Rapid turnover of both leaders and followers reduces the time people have to build up allegiances to wise, reassuring, and charismatic leaders. Automation of tasks and processes sweeps away whole occupations and professions—and the lifetimes of efforts at mastery that go with them. The proliferation of stakeholders with competing, even contradictory claims on the organization and growing stakeholder power ensure that single-minded commitment to one mission will be hard if not impossible to achieve. The rapid rise of foreign ownership coupled with leveraged buyouts where organizations are viewed as asset pools to be harvested signal clearly that organizations cannot and will not be valued in the future by their members and stakeholders the same way they were in the past. Security of employment essentially disappeared in the 1980s as a source of positive meaning, with attendant trauma. (Perhaps it is not so much the *fact* of unemployment that many workers, especially knowledge workers, feel, but the shock—the blow to their sense of order and meaning—of discovering that layoffs of valued, exemplary employees could happen at all.)

Stresses on meaning have also resulted from continuing discoveries about pollution and its effects on human health and the realization that these discoveries have made no organization safe from having its definition of itself questioned on legal, moral, biological, and ethical grounds. The experiences of the oil and cigarette companies, and the demise of Johns-Manville because of its inability to adapt to medical evidence about asbestos, are not isolated examples; they are paradigmatic.

Beyond local events in particular organizations, the last two decades have begun to see the crumbling of the institutions on which organizations depend for their existence—institutions like banks, the telephone system, ground and air transportation, state and local government, the school system, and the traditional family. Perturbations and crises in these external systems have undercut any given organization's internal efforts to create stable grounds of meaning. Continuing degradation of the national infrastructure may be the most vexing and baffling system of trends for practicing managers in the 1990s, with even so heretofore unthinkable an event as the financial collapse of the U.S. government by no means an impossibility.

Thus, the question of the grounds of coherence is of utmost importance, for in all these changes of form and function, high-quality human attitudes, actions, and feelings of various kinds are as important as ever for the viability of organizations. Indeed, as the stable systems on which we have counted for meaning fall into disarray, high-quality human attitudes and actions become more strategic than ever. Mediocre personal action only works when there is enough wisdom and momentum in the established system to fill in behind the ineffective actions of individuals. Furthermore, it appears that the grounds of coherence will themselves be matters of ongoing evolution, and therefore the question will be problematic for the foreseeable future.

The Possibility of Spiritual Grounding

Among the various modes of grounds of coherence I have mentioned, spirituality seems to point in a direction that is of renewed interest to many organization members as well as to consultants and theorists. However, the meaning of *spirituality* is itself very unclear. Confusion about the term's meaning comes from a powerful compound of strong but heterogeneous Judeo-Christian religious traditions and approaches, a burgeoning "new age" movement in which spirituality of some kind plays a central part, and a new interest in traditional non-Judeo-Christian religions and theologies. Furthermore, in the West all this positive interest and fervor exists in perpetual tension with the tradition of religious freedom, with its accompanying suspicion that anyone who wants to discuss spirituality may secretly have some proselytizing to do, some souls to save.

Spirituality—Some Working Distinctions

This intense compound of traditions and attitudes makes spirituality almost undiscussable in groups where the various belief systems of the members are unknown. It feels risky and awkward, and the point of doing it is always in question. The point of doing it here flows directly from the discussion in the preceding section about the loss of the grounds of meaning in organizations. Spirituality is considered here as a possible new direction for many who have not considered it before. However, a few further comments on the meaning of the term are in order before discussing its possible role in providing coherence and meaning in organizational life.

Definitional precision may be necessary at some point, but for the purposes of this chapter I am primarily concerned with what organization members mean when they talk about their interest in the spiritual aspects of life, especially those in the organization. *It really is a search for meaning that we can see going on.* In view of the stresses I have noted, though, it is a search that may have to go outside the official logic and the authoritative personages of the organization itself. The search is occasioned because our need for meaning is not satisfied by the various physical and material facts, events, and experiences of our organizational lives. Indeed, far from being satisfied, meaning needs are chronically frustrated in millions of organization members because of the trends and events discussed earlier in this chapter. "Meaning needs" is perhaps an unusual phrase, but this chapter assumes that such needs are felt as real by the person and are observable by third parties.

Spirituality and Meaning Needs

One of our fundamental problems of living is to find ways of meeting our ongoing meaning needs. We are tempted to try to settle them once and for all in various ways. A common method for adults in the contemporary world is to let the significance of the work we do in the organization we work for provide the grounds of meaning in our lives. These foundations, as already suggested, are increasingly in question. The occupational-organizational strategy is no longer as meaning-full as it once was.

Another very common strategy lies not in the value of what we do or who we work for but in what we have and can appear to be. We use such external props as certificates of achievement; money and material goods; physical attractiveness; power over others; association with celebrated people; sex, alcohol, and other drugs; and countless other things to provide meaning for us. There is nothing especially wrong with any of these as *pleasures;* it is when we seek to use them as our grounds for the meaning of our lives that their inadequacy becomes clear. As their possible inadequacy and harmfulness emerge we may deny this and cling to these props or even intensify our efforts toward them. If they are inadequate, though, chronic frustration of our meaning needs occurs, and this results in chronic fear and anxiety. We then may cling even more desperately to the props or run frantically from one to another seeking relief. We obsess about the props and hoard and use them compulsively. Some of the props are psychologically and even physically addictive, and when our reliance on a prop for meaning reaches this stage, we are moving beyond chronic fear and anxiety and into an actual life-threatening condition.

The question at this point is where to turn, for much twentieth-century psychotherapy and existentialist philosophy would agree so far that these patterns are pervasive in Western society. (This and the following four paragraphs appear with minor changes in Vaill, 1996, pp. 179–180). Spirituality is a decision to search somewhere else than in scientific findings and derived practices, secular support systems, or positive addictions like aerobic exercise, or in any other doctrines and technologies of human origin that purport to offer answers. Spirituality seeks fundamentally to get beyond materialist conceptions of meaning.

Spirituality is a decision to search beyond what one can do *to* and/or *on* and/or *within* oneself. It perceives the inadequacy to fundamentally lie not in the external props but in the self that would do the propping! Thus, to be spiritual is to try to turn away from all the props entirely and to open oneself to a transcendent source of meaning. Here at this act of opening, of course, is where all the theological and religious debates of human history begin. Obviously, I am not going to resolve any of these debates here. I can only locate them relative to the subject of spirituality.

To call this turning away from the material props a search, and to remember that it is being conducted by individuals, results in a view of spirituality as a personal process, a process occurring over time, expressing at any moment the individual's sense of the meaning of his or her life, of what the important questions are, of the significance of people and things around the individual, and of the direction in which the journey is going. To call it a personal process means that the debates *will* occur, for no two of us have the same meaning needs or will seek to open ourselves to the transcendent in quite the same way.

But the debates can be dialogue, as theologians seem increasingly to have discovered over the past quarter century. Spirituality does not need to be a matter of win-lose communication. We know that the end of that road is persecutions, religious wars, profound hatreds, and destruction of spiritual consciousness itself. None of this impugns spirituality, though; instead it impugns the tendency to fall back into the material ways of the world to prop up one's spiritual discoveries and realizations.

In this view, genuine spirituality must be the willingness to enter into the process of dialogue within oneself and with others, to try to stay with it over a period of time, and to remember that no one is going to find a once-and-for-all answer that warrants enforced universal adherence. What this amounts to is learning to think and communicate theologically—something, unfortunately, that is not presently contemplated for any known MBA program. It is a mentality that becomes increasingly important, though, as more and more people become spiritually active.

Spiritual Dialogue in Organizations

Several trends that are presently apparent in organizations may support the view of spirituality sketched above. There is a new interest in ethics, both academically and among practicing managers. Organizational credos and statements of basic beliefs, or "core values," as many managers call them, are appearing widely. New attention is being paid to the role of vision, viewed not as a technical recipe or strategic plan but rather as an inspired account of a desirable mode of organizational "being-in-the-world." There is continuing interest in stress management and genuine wellness, including the growing consensus that a self-destructive lifestyle is as much a spiritual problem as a medical or behavioral problem. Interest continues in philosophies and methods that help people to rediscover their connectedness to each other and their implication in each other's lives. People may turn away from viewing the organization as merely an instrument for attaining short-term financial objectives, at least as seen in such reformulations as Etzioni's *The Moral Dimension* (1988). The role philosophy and religion play in the thinking and actions of Asian managers is being explored. There is a powerful pulse of interest in twelve-step programs, with their explicit assertion of the spiritual emptiness that accompanies all compulsive-addictive behavior patterns, and an as yet relatively weak interest in taking care of the Earth (the Gaia movement), which quite likely will gather strength of sheer necessity as well as because of its felt spiritual validity. "Godless Communism" has collapsed, with a reawakening of public spirituality among millions who were denied it. And the approach of the year 2000 will likely fuel a reflective turn that for millions will have an actual apocalyptic aspect.

These trends and forces all contain the possibility of spiritual dialogue if they are seen as efforts to make organizations more meaningful to human beings with meaning needs. I may not have emphasized this point sufficiently: meaning is in the eye of the beholder, and the felt meaning of an organization's conduct will exist in relation to the meaning needs perceivers bring to that conduct. Many of these trends can be seen as responses to the ongoing organizing demands we are making of organizations; indeed, these more transcendental interests probably fuel the more practical changes we are trying to make in organizations. Not all of these forces and trends are equally spiritual, but a loose coalescence is gradually occurring and spirituality as a shared search for meaning may well become a more and more fundamental organizing process.

Not only do all of these trends have an impact on organizations; many of them also relate directly to the main mission. Not surprisingly, a question that always arises when considering the relation of spirituality to practical affairs is whether practical affairs will be conducted more successfully and effectively if they are infused with spiritual awareness. The question usually comes up in a somewhat loaded, "prove it to me" form. As far as is known, the potential efficacy of spirituality for secular goals can't be proven on the front end, and it probably is a distortion of spiritual concern itself to insist that it prove itself in this way. As I have suggested, the spiritual search results in a progressive transformation of the felt meaning of life and experience. The exact same organizational results may look very different to an enlightened consciousness as compared with a less enlightened one. Seemingly "lesser" results happening to a spiritually developed person may be experienced by the person as greater, more valuable, more enlightening, and basically more satisfying than they would seem to a person who is less spiritually aware.

And so to one who asks, "How will my life be better as a result of working on the spiritual aspects of things? Will my organization be more effective and profitable?" the only answer that can be given at the outset is "As you proceed, your question will change its meaning for you and you will become comfortable with whatever results you attain." Acceptance of that answer is the basic act of faith that spiritual exploration requires.

I have not mentioned it thus far, but this may be the place to note that it is also possible that a real Unseen Other is participating in and amplifying the forces and trends that reflect the spiritual search. However, belief in the intervention of an Unseen Other is not necessary to a consideration of the human implications of these things, nor does this chapter take a position pro or con on the question of the possibility of divine action in the world. This is because spirituality really only needs to transcend the material world. It is not mandatory that it presume at the outset conceptions of spiritual truths and/or beings that possess qualities of divine character or infinite magnitude. My own experience is that our spiritual conception grows with spiritual practice; our idea about the nature of the divine grows, changes, and deepens as part of our spiritual growth.

Respiritualizing the Psyche

Increasingly, for better or worse, formal work organizations can be and are being framed as spiritual places. The search for meaning is being carried into a spiritual realm. Less and less will it be possible to understand organizational behavior without understanding the role of spirituality in human thinking, feeling, and action. *We are engaged in nothing less than a "respiritualizing of the psyche."* Among other things, this means that we will need to revisit the writings of the theologians, social critics, and psychotherapists who have been saying for years that we need to respiritualize the psyche. Indeed, a new literature will doubtless evolve that is more directly focused on organizational life. It is extraordinary how much consideration has actually been given to spirituality in human affairs over the centuries, even though one would never realize this from perusing the contemporary management literature.

Organizational Inquiry and Spiritual Search

The above remarks carry another set of implications entirely for those who study human behavior in organizations. The question is, how are concepts like meaning needs and spiritual dialogue to be approached as empirical phenomena? The position I take is that whether this question is taken seriously depends in large part on the condition of the meaning needs of the person who is asking the question. The more an investigator has personally moved through the experience of loss of meaning that this chapter has discussed and the more he or she is open to the spiritual as a possible source of more resilient meaning, the easier it will be for that person to observe and interpret these same processes in organization members. Conversely, all that has been said can be easily dismissed by someone who is convinced that contemporary academic grounds of meaning are perfectly adequate for living in the world and inquiring further into the human condition.

There is, of course, considerable current debate on whether academic approaches to organizational life *are* adequately founded. Positivistic objectivity and precision and adherence to canons of inquiry drawn from other than the human sciences have come under heavy criticism in the past two decades, partly precisely because the study of such phenomena as the human need for meaning tends to be ruled out. Many investigators have a dawning conviction that far deeper and more agonizing feelings and pursuits are going on among people in organizations than rigorous scientific inquiry is able to notice.

It is not clear how our understanding of organizational behavior may change as the spiritual condition of the observer changes. The preferred hypothesis is that a fuller understanding of human nature occurs as the spiritual consciousness of the observer grows richer. Enormous anecdotal evidence exists to support this hypothesis, if the wise sayings of spiritually enlightened individuals over the centuries are considered. A more modest and perhaps more pointed question for contemporary readers of this chapter is not whether we are going to compete with the great theologians and mystics in our insights, but whether we are going to be in the game at all. If we only hold ourselves responsible for *findings*, letting *meanings* go for some other time and some other interpreter, we will not ask the questions that will help us to understand the spiritual needs of today's organizational inhabitants, nor will we be able to learn what there is to be learned from the mystical insights of earlier ages.

Conclusion

Thus, from the widespread phenomenon of the loss of meaning in organizational life, we find that meaning needs may be seen in the experience of spirituality. This chapter asserts that spirituality is becoming an interesting and attractive alternative source of meaning in today's organizations. In order to perceive this, it is suggested that we need to overcome the disincentives to discussing spirituality and, further, that the spiritual condition of investigators also comes into play, for they too have their experience of the assaults on meaning of the modern world. The spiritual condition of theorists and researchers of human phenomena is a bit beyond the scope of this chapter, but it seems clear that their spiritual condition must be part of any consideration of how to look at organizations as inherently spiritual places.

10

Spirituality in the Age of the Leveraged Buyout

The main thrust of this chapter is as follows: it is said that there is a fundamental dislocation between our everyday lives and what we choose to call the spiritual life. I am concerned, professionally, with the leadership and management of all kinds of organizations—and have been for twenty-five years, my first faculty position having commenced on July 1, 1964, at the UCLA Graduate School of Management. The faith I act on is that it *is* possible to lead a spiritual life at work in a typical Western organization, be it public or private, profit or nonprofit, large or small, successful or unsuccessful. Some of us might say a bit sarcastically, "Well, of *course* it has to be possible. How else could you keep your sanity and keep your body and soul together in a typical organization if you weren't able to lead a spiritual life, to some extent anyway?" I don't disagree with that way of putting it, for indeed organizations can seem to be pretty crazy places, testing our survival skills at the most fundamental level. The spiritual life is a good way of hanging on, you might say.

Note: Keynote address for the conference "Spirituality in Life and Work," Georgetown University, School for Summer and Continuing Education, Washington, D.C., July 21, 1989.

This, though, is not the way I want to come at the question. Yes, a more spiritual life can be a kind of last resort when all else has failed, but I don't want to restrict it to that. I want to show that human organizations are inherently spiritual places where, far from a spiritual life being a matter of survival and self-protection entered into reluctantly and in desperation, a spiritual life is *invited* by human organizations. Indeed, the more I reflect on it the more it seems to me that without a willingness to try to lead a more spiritual life, we cannot understand what is going on in a human organization, we will not be able to see very clearly how to be personally effective there, and we won't get much personal pleasure out of being there. Even worse—and here is the radical implication of the approach I want to explore—I believe that if we can't see how to lead a spiritual life in relation to our typical Western organizations, we are not going to be able to lead a spiritual life *at all*. There really is no place to hide, to be blunt about it, no extraorganizational place to be more spiritual than seems to be possible in everyday organizations.

Tempting Escapes

It might be possible to escape from the specific craziness of a specific organization in a specific place and time, but not from organizational life in general. Various escapes do tempt us, of course. Communes in Vermont seem to offer peace and tranquillity, but as thousands found out in the 1960s, communes are still organizations, some of the small towns they are situated near are too, and they are therefore saturated with everyday conflicts and dilemmas. Small business is no escape, for your employees still expect you to be "organized," and if they don't your landlord, your banker, and your customers certainly do. Acquiring a batch of advanced degrees and some kind of professional certification is not a defense either: you are still going to be an employee or a partner or a proprietor and as a result your professional degree merely qualifies you to be frustrated with your organization in a more specialized and sophisticated way.

Promotion to higher levels is believed by many to bring relief from organizational craziness, but that doesn't work either, despite the folklore. Instead, higher levels primarily bring greater pressure, higher stakes, deeper predicaments, and greater costs of mistakes.

One possibly promising avenue of hope is all the organizations that are consciously trying to be more spiritual places. I have been in many such organizations as a leader, member, client, and consultant. I must say that I don't find them more naturally, automatically felicitous places for spiritual life than other, less spiritually conscious and spiritually ambitious organizations.

Recently I had the opportunity to speak to a conference put on by such a consciously spiritual organization. The conference theme was warmly spiritual. The audience could not have been more ready to listen and participate. But getting from the airport to the conference, lost on back streets at midnight in a thunderstorm, was not a spiritual experience at all. The hall I was to speak in was a public cafeteria with all the attendant background sound effects. The group was smaller than I had expected and the sound system did not work too well. These are all organizational issues: this organization's spiritual mission was no guarantee against practical difficulties and, to say the least, my capacity to lead a spiritual life in this assignment was severely tested. Fortunately, things worked out well: I made lots of new friends, gave what I'm told was a good talk, and have decided to join the organization and participate regularly in its activities. The organizational stresses were not trivial, though, and it would not have been wise to pretend to ignore them. (Part of leading a spiritual life in an organization, I think, is to pay attention to and work through the feelings one has about various organizational events such as these. I say that as one who has tried for years to make the stiff-upper-lip, feelings-don't-matter strategy work and failed.)

Retirement is a final matter I will mention in this illustrative catalog. It also is no escape from organizational absurdities. In retirement, we just have more time to gnash our teeth about the impact of organizations on us—our landlord, our church, the hospital, the supermarket, the Social Security Administration, or any of the dozens of other systems that seem to become more complex, mysterious, and threatening as we grow older. Just in passing, since I am talking about retirement, I might note that movies like Warren Beatty's *Heaven Can Wait* and Michael Keaton's *Beetlejuice*, as well as countless jokes about St. Peter at Heaven's gate and cartoons of angels standing around on clouds, suggest that even after we die all kinds of organizational issues are awaiting us in the afterlife. The faithful are promised eternal life in many religions. You don't suppose that this means eternal *organizational* life, do you?

The point is that we can't get away from organizational events that challenge our feelings, our sense of wholeness, and our self-respect. We can't get away from red tape, from delays, from bureaucratic functionaries who treat us like a number, from the seeming coldness and ruthlessness of the higher-ups or the anger and resentfulness of the lower-downs, from the waste and confusion, from the sometimes horrifying, life-destroying mistakes that are often made. The *Challenger* disaster was caused more by organizational problems than technical problems. There was nothing wrong with the *Exxon Valdez* technically but a lot wrong in its human systems. The Calvert Cliffs, Maryland, nuclear power plant, a mile from my house, has just had its whole top management replaced—not its reactors and other physical facilities. I have considered offering myself to them as a consultant, but then I wonder: do I want to know what I would find out as a consultant? I am honestly perplexed about this question.

If spiritual life is not possible in organizational life—here is the hard edge of my argument—then I reluctantly conclude that I must give up the idea of spiritual life, for I can't get away from organizations. However, I don't intend to give up the idea of trying to live a more spiritual life in a thoroughly organizational world; indeed, I refuse. I think there is another alternative, and in the remainder of this chapter I want to say what I think it is.

Personal Versus Organizational Focus

I had a basic choice to make here about the way to discuss the possibilities for a more spiritual life in a world pervaded by organizations. On the one hand, I could focus on what is involved in leading a more spiritual life as a matter of personal practice; alternatively, I could talk about organizations as settings for leading a more spiritual life. I have chosen the latter course—to try to rethink organizations as spiritual environments. The other focus has been much more thoroughly explored and there is a great deal of exciting, contemporary work going on. But this work cannot truly find application if we can't see organizations as environments where spiritual life is possible. Also, I feel my credentials are stronger to discuss new ways of looking at organizations than they are to discuss forms and methods of spiritual practice, for on this topic I am very much a beginner.

The somewhat cryptic title of this chapter, "Spirituality in the Age of the Leveraged Buyout," can be easily explained in the light of this organizational focus I want to explore. A leveraged buyout is the purchase of an organization—usually a for-profit organization—by buyers who usually obtain their funds through quite high-interest debt, sometimes called junk bonds. The reason the buyers (who sometimes are the organization's own management) are willing to commit themselves to huge debt obligations is that they believe that if they can get control of the company, they can generate large cash flows that will pay off the debt and leave them with a large capital gain through an increase in the stock price or through the sale of assets. Sometimes we hear that the company is to be "broken up," sometimes that assets will be "spun off" or "harvested"—but it comes to the same thing: an abrupt, radical intervention is made into the affairs of the company for the purpose of relieving the debt burden the new owners have taken on to gain control. The term *leverage* merely refers to the way a very small commitment of one's own money (as opposed to what is borrowed) can "pry" large returns from the company.

I will interrupt myself briefly to say that some buyouts occur because the buyers want to run the company and believe they can do it more effectively with a different governance and management structure. I am not concerned here with that type of takeover, provided it is done legally, because the buyers' motives are to do the organization's job better than it is presently being done—not to terrorize and exploit, but to lead and develop.

In the "get control, sell off, get out" type of buyout, which we have seen proliferate enormously in the 1980s, the buyers are not concerned with whom they hurt as they pry on the organization's resources. Their view is exploitative; they are raiders. They treat the organization as a financial object, as a "cash cow," to use the phrase from a popular model of strategic choice, a material thing that exists only to be an instrument for those who are strong enough to get control of it. This human setting, in other words, this actual community of vision and feeling, is treated as nothing but a money machine.

For the sake of clarity and brevity, I will henceforth refer to this view as the *material-instrumental* (or M-I) model of an organization: *material* because the organization is deemed to have no reality or meaning beyond the financial value of its physical assets (including its people, who are viewed as material "human resources" or a "talent pool") and *instrumental* because it is deemed to exist only to achieve the objectives that those who own it set for it.

The M-I model is the dominant model of what an organization is in Western culture. It is 250 years old, at least. It is applied to all kinds of organizations, not just for-profit corporations. It is so deep in our cultural consciousness that many of us can no longer see that it *is* a model. To millions of us, it is not a model but just the way organizations are, period. Even people whose lives have been profoundly harmed by the corporate raiders' practice of this model have trouble saying what is wrong with the model and what alternatives, if any, there are. They may feel that there should be an alternative but they can't say what it may be. Sometimes, though, we are pushed to extreme rejection of the private, for-profit organization as such—a doctrine we call in America socialism or Marxism. Total rejection is possible, of course, but before I start tossing Molotov cocktails at our Western organizations, I want to see if we can't rethink the M-I model in a little less drastic way. Recall that we are still looking for a way to make it easier to see how an organization can be an invitation to greater spiritual awareness and practice, rather than a soul-destroying money machine.

An Instructive Thought Experiment

Let me suggest a little thought experiment. I would like you to think about the best experience you have ever had in an organization— the most memorable experience, the one that you look back on most fondly, that you enjoy thinking and talking about, even bragging about. It doesn't matter what kind of an organization it was or is, how important its mission, or how famous or successful it was or is by the world's standards. Some people I ask this question of are presently in the best situation they have ever been in, but many are not. Some hark back to college, their adolescence, or even childhood. Some mention their families, but most do not. For some it is a sports experience; men often mention military experiences. Voluntary organizations such as fund-raising groups, political campaigns, or charities often get mentioned, as do performing arts troupes.

I am going to pause for a couple of minutes while you decide on the experience and reflect on it in as much detail as you can. Then I will ask you to briefly discuss with the person sitting next to you what the experience was and what it meant to you.

———————

So. There is my proof that spiritual life is practical in organizational contexts. You see, I know what you talked about with each other— not the facts, of course, but the feelings and the character of the experience. (And I might even be able to guess at a few facts that would be close to some of your examples.)

My experience with others who have done what I have asked you to do leads me to think you have remembered the following kinds of things:

- You recalled how valuable you felt the work you were doing was at the time you were doing it, and the quality, even the true art, with which you and the others involved were doing it.

- You remembered how strong the teamwork was and how often it bordered on virtual love of the others in the group.

- Many of you recalled what extraordinary leadership existed in the situation and said that these leaders were people with an incredible capacity to scrounge resources, cut through confusion, deal with external threats, and keep people feeling positive and enthusiastic.

- In one way or another, your situations exhibited the unusual ability of a group to pursue objectives through thick and thin, stay on track, and stay committed.

- Many of your situations were cause for much comment by those around the group but not in it, and not all of the comment was friendly or admiring.

- One of the things you may have remembered most vividly is how you were transformed when you were in this situation, how you were almost lifted onto another plane of existence. You like yourself as you were then. You may have wondered since why you can't be like that more of the time.

I think you can be like that more of the time, but unlike that situation, which perhaps emerged spontaneously, it is more common for the spontaneous magic *not* to be happening and for us to find ourselves in the position of needing to help it happen—or wishing that we could *make* it happen! Our temptation—good children of the M-I culture that we are—is to try to engineer the magic, program it, make it happen, fundamentally to call forth excellence by the optimal organization of the material resources we think we have. But fostering organizational conditions and events where people have the feelings and experiences you have just been reflecting on is not an engineering problem. The reason it isn't is that human beings are not material instruments. That isn't a good model of what human beings are in their relatively natural state. Of course, human beings aren't stupid either, and we know that if we apply enough naked force to human beings, they will fulfill the M-I model, the robot model, that we want them to.

However, when we do this the human being's natural inclination not to be a robot assumes a new form; a new motive arises—one he or she did not have before we came along with our naked force. The additional motive becomes that of evading the naked force! We know that the human being is endlessly inventive in acting on this motive. Among the more common methods of evading force are physically leaving the situation, shutting down sullenly, becoming pathetically compliant and obsequious, or perhaps most tragically by deciding that if life is going to be a matter of the application of naked force everywhere, it is far better to be the for*cer* than the for*cee*, so the thing to do is to set about getting some clout for oneself. Thereby hangs the tale of the motive for a lot of career planning.

Fostering transcendent experiences isn't an engineering problem. We do not call forth the best from people, including ourselves, by naked force, by threat, or by subtle manipulation. We do not foster sustainable high-quality thought and action from the outside by pulling on strings and trying to arrange optimal conditions and incentive structures.

Well then, how do we do it? How do situations like the ones you all have in your own experience occur? Let me take you back to those situations for a minute. It is clear that the M-I model does not capture them. Look at yourself in that situation: you were not just "doing a job." You were not manipulated to perform at the level you achieved. You weren't just doing it for the money, although you may have started out thinking you were. But that is not what became your main sense of yourself in that situation, nor is it the sense that other people had of you. In fact, many people are rather astonished, looking back, at how much they did with no thought to the material rewards that might come to them. Therein lies a mystery that 100 years of secular psychology have yet to explain.

Organizations as Valuing Systems

One thing we often discover when we reflect on ourselves in those situations is that we weren't doing what we were doing for just one reason, but out of a complex of reasons: belief in the purpose or goal of the activity, liking and friendship for the others, pleasure in the exercise and development of our own skills and feelings for the activity, admiration and loyalty and maybe awe of the leader, maybe a sense of being part of and contributing to a tradition, maybe the fact that we made a promise or took an oath. A whole system of values was at play in our awareness and feeling for ourselves, and it was a *system* in our awareness and not just a list. Further, I hope you will not consider it too long a stretch to assume that the others in the situation were having an equally complex and perhaps ineffable experience. Sometimes you made eye contact with them at a crucial moment or otherwise had the clear realization that it meant as much to them as it did to you.

This realization is not so unusual; the human being is rarely purely single-minded. The essence of our conscious human action is its multifunctionality. In more down-to-earth terms, we routinely keep several balls in the air at once or kill several birds with one stone.

So our motives, values, and reasons were complex. We know that our immediate colleagues' reasons were complex. And our sense of what the overall experience was for—its purpose—was complex. While there may have been one or two official goals or bottom lines, many kinds of excellence were displayed in the situation, not just one. Occasionally, in a burst, everything may have had to be sacrificed to one overriding goal, but looking back we can see that a variety of things got routinely taken care of and that all-out sacrifice for one goal does not describe the actual quality of the situation.

From the perspective of having studied lots of such situations, I am able to say that this experience is widely shared. At a concrete level, it is each person's thoroughly subjective experience of a unique, particular situation. But when the same subjective experience begins to show up over and over in connection with a particular mode of life and performance of a human grouping, I begin to suspect that we are on to something that is more than personal and subjective, something that is existential in human experience and in human beings.

What is that? How do we describe a human grouping that is managing to provide its members with an intense, positive, memorable experience, an experience that is for each utterly real yet somewhat ineffable, that is for each plain as day yet at bottom somewhat mysterious, that is clearly *happening* but that cannot be said to be consciously engineered, planned, or managed? First of all I suggest—and here we move past the M-I model—that we are observing a *valuing* system. We are observing an ongoing process wherein this thing we call an organization is managing to be a place where members are having the positive experiences I have been discussing. You don't hear that very often—that an organization is a value system or a *valuing* system to preserve the dynamic. We say that a person has a value system and engages in valuing, but we don't say that organizations are value systems. Why don't we? We don't, I think, because the M-I model leads us away from values and disguises them with words like "resources" and "priorities" and "constraints"; furthermore, it takes them out of the stream of time and treats them as fixed, static things. Further, the M-I model views the organization as someone's instrument, not as itself a valuing system.

Unconscious Abstractions

So, in the M-I model, an organization *has* resources, priorities, and constraints, but it is hard to see how it got that way because of this unconscious double abstraction that has been made: first, singularity out of multiplicity, and second, fixity out of flow and change. We create single values out of the infinite permutations and shadings of values that human beings are capable of evolving and experiencing, and then we freeze these single values into things that we treat as timeless and unchanging. The M-I model rests, in other words, on a model of values and valuing that is psychologically absurd and bankrupt.

In fact, a third abstraction is performed by splitting each personal consciousness off from the thing that is valued and treating the thing as valuable independent of those who perceive it as valuable: splitting profit from the profiteer, teamwork from the team, beauty from the eye of the beholder. The M-I model can only stand up as long as we accept this triple abstraction: single value out of the value manifold, valu*e* out of valu*ing*, and value as object out of value as subject-object union. I am sorry to be so abstract, but it is at this level that we have to chop at the M-I monolith if we are to see a role for our spiritual practice and spiritual development.

A Five-Way Bottom Line

After a great deal of inspecting and reflecting upon the good experiences that people do have in organizations, I have concluded that it is possible to talk about five ongoing, intertwined streams of valuing—a "five-way bottom line," if you will, that never stays still. (This idea of a five-way bottom line is also discussed from a somewhat different point of view in Vaill, 1989, chap. 3.) My alternative to the M-I model is a view of the organization as this five-dimensional, intertwined stream where the *energy* that keeps it all going comes from the individual and joint actions of people as they work out their sense of what is important, of what things they need to do in their own present reality to fulfill and continue to pursue their sense of who they are. The five categories or dimensions, I hasten to say, are simple and easily recognizable. I call them the *economic*, the *technical*, the *communal*, the *adaptive*, and the *transcendent*.

By the *economic* I mean all the actions (acts of valuing) one can see in an organization that have to do with saving resources, using them wisely, making a profit, cutting costs, and generally being conscious of the value of resources. A huge amount of valuing is subsumed within this category. It is the primary conscious value of the M-I model.

By the *technical* I mean all the actions (acts of valuing) one can see having to do with the way the organization does its work—all the emphasis on method, on efficiency, on craft, on quality, on keeping up with the state of the art, on innovating and inventing new approaches. This is the category of the great American value of know-how. The M-I model calls this category *operations* and treats its contents purely as means to economic ends. However, you don't have to look very hard to see that craft and quality and efficiency easily become ends in themselves for someone who cares about the activity. Herein lies the eternal tension between what is good enough to sell and what is always capable of improvement.

By the *communal* I mean all the valuing we do of each other in our organizational lives, all the emphasis on teamwork, all the spontaneous acts of helping, all that we do to try to manage conflict, to communicate clearly and respectfully to others. It is what German sociologists in the early twentieth century called the mode of gemeinschaft—the family feeling, the bonds and norms of groups one is a member of. In the M-I model, little value is placed on the events in this category. There may be a grudging admission that people have social needs, but there will be a constant return to the bottom line as defined by the economic category. "We only care about teams to the extent that they improve productivity," says the

M-I model. Sadly, we are hearing just this chant in the otherwise impressive employee involvement movement that so many companies are a part of.

What I call the *adaptive* acts of valuing consist of all the things an organization does to be a good citizen in its environment, all the relationships it tends, all the ways it devotes time and energy to managing its boundaries. Again, this is a category of values that the M-I model will only admit to the extent that it affects the financial bottom line. The mainstream strategic management field—a latter-day apostle of the M-I model—calls actions in this category *stakeholder relationships* and places a lot of importance on understanding one's stakeholders: suppliers, customers, employees, community, and so forth. What is often forgotten by the M-I model, though, is that you don't unilaterally define your stakeholders. They define themselves in relation to you. It is up to them, not you alone, to perceive the stake they have in you. If the organization only adapts to the stakeholders *it* defines, it is going to be unprepared for, and may consider illegitimate, claims by stakeholders it has not voluntarily noticed.

Evidence for the strategic management field's one-sided view of adaptation lies in its fascination with the phrase "environmental scanning," as if the viewing only goes one way. In fact, the stakeholders are scanning too! A better model of the whole process of adaptation is *diplomacy*, where there is an ongoing interaction of interests and proposals. But diplomacy is too messy and contingent for those schooled in the arrogance of the M-I model. It has taught them that they need only be interested in their environment to the extent that it is clearly and immediately relevant to their own pursuits.

The final category of valuing is the *transcendent*, which consists of all the acts of valuing you can see in an organization that have to do with creating meaning for people, meaning that is satisfying to human consciousness and human feeling. Sociologists have shown repeatedly how real and important, indeed indispensable, the sense-making process is, even though this notion has not yet penetrated the popular mind and certainly has not disturbed the M-I model very much. But it is our transcendent values and perceptions that permit us to critique things like the M-I model itself! As a model it is dogmatic, not reflectively open. It does not want anyone looking in the organization for any deeper or higher meanings beyond getting the job done in the most expeditious way possible. The M-I model ignores the fact that the very human beings whose actions it seeks to model contain as part of their essence the tendency to look for deeper or higher meanings!

Furthermore, not only is there ongoing sense making and meaning making; these processes are truly transcendent because they go well beyond objective facts and reflect our hopes, yearnings, fears, and other passions. They do not usually consist of calm, cool assessment but are instead intensely human. The transcendent is a category of values because these activities are important to us—we will fight for the right to our meanings and interpretations and for the opportunity to engage in the process with others. Isn't it interesting? In every organization there is intense, nonstop discussion of the meaning of the organization, occurring both officially and unofficially, and the M-I model is relatively oblivious to all of it. Fifty years after research began to show that every organization has a lively grapevine of merry meaning makers, those who believe in the M-I model still can't come to terms with it and want there to be only one official version of what is happening. This can be seen today in many of the well-meaning attempts to clarify the organization's mission, with heavy emphasis on what the organization's leadership wants. After all, since the organization is top management's instrument, it is only natural that top management should articulate its vision and then sell it to everyone else—only natural, anyway, in the logic of the M-I model.

But the transcendent belongs to everyone because it is a natural human tendency. In the networks and matrix structures that modern organizations are evolving, this omnidirectional meaning making can be seen quite clearly. In such organizations the transcendent has to be seen as an end in itself. The fact that in many networked organizations this is not yet realized and meaning continues to be imposed from the top helps me to understand why many networks and matrix structures work so poorly.

Spiritual Practice in a Multivaluing System

You might expect that I am getting ready to argue that this transcendent category is where our spiritual life and development best find their expression. I would certainly agree that the ways in which we go about interpreting the people and events around us reflect our spiritual condition and level of spiritual development. But I don't want to restrict or sequester our spiritual life to that "soft" area of organizational valuing. I can just hear some hard-nosed, bottom-line-oriented devotee of the M-I model say, "You folks can have all the mystical conversations you want, just so it doesn't get in the way of getting the work out."

In fact, this *is* the history of valuing in both the communal and transcendent categories as expressed in the field known as organization development. The M-I model dismisses these concerns as "touchy-feely" and therefore of only trivial importance to organizational success. I might note in passing, though, that the tough-minded advocates of the M-I model talk differently when their own spiritual needs and spiritual pain are being discussed. Every pastoral counselor knows this well—that the tough-minded bluster often changes quite dramatically in a spiritual crisis. Of course, too often it changes right back when the crisis is over. But not always.

No, it is not just within the transcendent category that I locate our spiritual life and possibilities. We need to learn to look in all five. Let me say what talking about the organization as an ongoing valuing system of five intertwined themes comes to for our spiritual life. Remember, the five intertwined themes are themselves abstractions—the feelings and acts of valuing we actually see are much more concrete and specific.

I suggest that we can think of *each* of these categories and their interrelations, and the myriad of specifics behind them, in spiritual terms. Isn't it interesting that despite all the decades, even centuries, of fulminating by the M-I model about the need for single-minded devotion to just one value, this manifold of values continues to appear and be felt as real and significant by us. These values are *there*; they have existential validity despite the protestations of the M-I model. Now you can perhaps see more clearly why I made the somewhat startling statement at the beginning of this chapter that "without a willingness to try to lead a more spiritual life, we cannot understand what is going on in a human organization, we will not be able to see very clearly how to be personally effective there, and we won't get much personal pleasure out of being there." The value of the five categories is that they give us some focus and a modest framework with which to discuss what our spiritual life might look like. What truly are the values in each category and why are they important to us? That is the question that opens toward our spiritual feeling and awareness and level of spiritual development.

For the purposes of this chapter, the spiritual meaning of each category can only be sketched. But clearly it is the next main piece of business if we are serious about recovering the possibilities for spiritual life in organizations.

In the economic category, a progressive spiritual awareness might be concerned with the true human meaning of waste, of loss, of so-called ill-gotten gains and windfalls. Debt and living beyond one's means come to have moral meaning. The profligacy with which the Bible is so frequently concerned becomes something to eliminate in one's attitudes and actions. Several of the Seven Deadly Sins are actually concerned with what you might call uneconomic behavior. Right there on the M-I model's front porch, so to speak, are matters of tremendous importance in spiritual life.

Within the technical category the notions of craft and of quality work seem to create virtually an unlimited field for spiritual life and learning. Respect for materials and the work of others could also be in this category. Commitment to one's growth as a craftsperson belongs here. Frequently this involves consideration of aesthetic values as well as utilitarian ones, and aesthetics provides a limitless field for spiritual growth.

The sense of fellowship that arises in the communal category hardly needs to have its spiritual meaning and value defended, except that with the noisy advocacies of the M-I model going on it is sometimes hard to hear the quieter statements of yearning for greater team feeling, the lonely calls echoing from one office to another in so many organizations. The spiritual value of human brotherhood and sisterhood; that is what I think this category is about.

The adaptive category has many applications. In general, boundaries frequently are self-reinforcing and the many varieties of groups, races, industries, professions, and sectors of society can get very out of touch. It takes enormous energy and courage to work across boundaries, as we can see in any labor strike, in the Middle East, and in Northern Ireland, for example. It is easy to let the adaptive values be someone else's problem. But I think that with increasing spiritual maturity, the value of strategic harmonizing of relationships across boundaries becomes more and more clear. Another way of saying this is that the adaptive category is the ability to keep your head in the organization when your stakeholders are making life miserable for you. Forbearance toward and forgiveness of obstreperous stakeholders? Heck no, says the M-I model. Sue 'em right back! If they spy on us, we spy on them. If they raid us, we raid them. Make them an offer they can't refuse. But what of the idea of turning the other cheek toward troublesome stakeholders. Does it seem radical? The M-I model would certainly say so, but any large institution, like a Harvard or an IBM, will tell you that they do it all the time.

Finally, in the transcendent category, I think one of the chief opportunities we have for spiritual life is in *helping* with the meaning making, helping it to become more than grousing and bellyaching, more than naysaying and cynicism, for all these modes rest on an interpretation that has been made of the situation. Some meaning making can be pretty irresponsible and even destructive, I think we would agree. Another avenue for our spiritual awareness in this category is the language with which we interpret the meaning of events in the organization. It is heavily psychological and sociological, pseudoscientific, full of questionable attributions of cause and effect, riddled with all-or-one thinking, and quite materialistic. Such a vocabulary and conceptual apparatus tends to produce interpretations that are negative, cynical, and reductionist. A sour hopelessness can come to pervade a whole organization's mentality. Our own growth—the helping I speak of—is in coming to learn to talk of spiritual matters in the organization in a way that is neither too archaic and pious-sounding nor too trendy and slick. It is actually a kind of ministry, I think, this business of helping others explore more spiritual interpretations of organizational events.

Conclusion

So there is a sketch of how our spiritual feelings pertain to the daily events and issues of our organizations. I hope I have demonstrated that, far from being marginal or irrelevant, spiritual values, energy, and faith are central to the organization's very survival and development.

Let me say one more thing about faith in relation to our spiritual life in organizations. You may have wondered, Where is God in all of this? Where are the specific doctrines and practices of religion? Nothing I have said is intended to downplay religious faith. However, the way I *would* put it is that my argument about spiritual life is relevant to a person whether or not he or she has a religious faith. Even the thoroughgoing atheist has values, has to deal with the multiplicity of values that operate, and has to continually reflect and try to grow in understanding these values and their interrelationships.

I confess that I *am* thinking of an audience with a faith in some kind of Divinity, but it does not have to be such an audience. In addition to my faith in my own version of God, I have another kind of faith relating to the doubters and the outright atheists. My faith is that if they think more and more about it, they will see that ultimately all values are grounded in an invisible, supernatural Something that can only be approached and experienced within what we call faith and through prayer. The key is to keep thinking about it and to keep asking the question. As the American philosopher Charles Hartshorne (1953, p. 177) has said, "If there is no universal mind in the cosmos, it has proved beyond the power of philosophy to state wherein the cosmic order consists. As Russell and Santayana and many others have admitted, the theoretical foundation of the scientist's trust in the reliability of discoverable natural uniformities is not apparent—apart, that is, from the theistic foundation which these men reject."

My own experience is that there is no upper limit to spiritual reflection, insight, and growth, and that in itself is an argument for the existence of Divinity. As we wrestle with the interrelations of all these values as they are concretely experienced and as they evolve and intertwine through time, it seems to me to become clearer why over the ages people have had revelations of the existence of all human works and all human institutions "under God," as we say. And that is why I think any organization, whether it is a global corporation, a huge government agency, a university, or just Al and Tony's Auto Body Shop, is a perfectly fine place in which to try to lead a spiritual life.

11

Executive Development as Spiritual Development

In the film *Lawrence of Arabia*, T. E. Lawrence (Peter O'Toole) has been sent into the desert to find the headquarters of Sharif Faisal (Alec Guinness). He meets Colonel Brighton (Anthony Quayle), who has come out from Faisal's camp to find Lawrence. Brighton is very skeptical of Lawrence's qualifications to be visiting Faisal. At one point, as they ride through the desert, he asks Lawrence, rather coolly, just what the British government's Arab Bureau back in Cairo expects him to do. Lawrence's answer is a perfect introduction to the central focus of this chapter. Somewhat apologetically, he replies that his job is rather vague, but that Cairo wants him to "appreciate the situation."

Lawrence does not yet know what leadership he will personally exert in the coming years with the Arabs. The Arabs for their part have little idea of how they will respond to Lawrence, or what they are truly capable of against the Turks. A deep process of the *discovery of spirit* goes on between Lawrence and his Arab compatriots. As such it is an archetype for a similar process that needs to go on between executives and the organizations they lead. Or, rather, it

---

Note: Originally published as a chapter in S. Srivastva, D. Cooperrider, and Associates, *Appreciative Management and Leadership: The Power of Positive Thought and Action in Organizations.* San Francisco: Jossey-Bass, 1990. Reprinted, slightly edited, with permission.

should be an archetype, but often it is not. Instead, the primary emphasis among contemporary writers seems to be exhortation of executives about the sense of mission, about the new vision, vitality, and spirit they are supposed to impart to their organizations. I see very little attention being given to the question of where this vision, vitality, and spirit are going to come from in the leader who is imparting them.

This then is the question addressed in this chapter: *What are the implications for the spiritual condition and the spiritual growth of individual executives of the need for them to foster vision, vitality, and spirit in the organizations they lead?* Stated not as a question but as a hypothesis, the subject of this chapter is the idea that, to a large extent, *executive development for leadership of modern organizations is spiritual development.*

There are a number of parts to the overall question. I must first summarize the significance for the *organization* of these ideas about vision, vitality, and spirit. This section will be relatively brief because there has been a great deal of discussion of these qualities already; I will assume that you are generally aware of the emphasis that has recently been placed on them. The second question is, What about the spiritual condition, present and future, of the men and women who are organization leaders? This is a difficult question and will only be addressed in a speculative and preliminary fashion here. It is also a subject on which we are all about equally informed and/or opinionated, and it is with considerable diffidence that I undertake a discussion of it at all.

The final section will discuss the process of spiritual development. It will raise some questions and offer some possibilities about how this might be done by those who are concerned with the spiritual condition of modern executives, including those executives themselves.

As one final word of introduction, I wish to say that I think the problems I am talking about here are the most important contemporary problems in management. I think it is a scandal that there should be so little discussion of them in the mainstream of management education and development. At best, we tend to treat the subject as primarily a matter of ethics. The practice of any system of ethics, though, makes all kinds of assumptions about the spiritual condition of those who are going to do the practicing. I am genuinely embarrassed for myself and my colleagues that we should, by and large, be leaving these deep questions of executive character unaddressed, all the while calling for new vision, vitality, and spirit in Western organizations. The book for which this chapter was originally prepared can only be described as an act of intellectual heroism—one that I fervently hope will have a lasting impact on the profession and be the first of a new genre.

Vision, Vitality, and Spirit

At the present time, the broadest topics that organization leaders are being encouraged to inject into their organizations are *mission* and *vision*. These at least are the two terms one hears over and over in executive seminars, in the opening chapters of books on strategic management, and in admiring accounts of how one executive or another achieved a dramatic turnaround. Among consultants and seminar leaders, the hottest subject these days is the vision workshop, and countless organization members are going through fairly carefully thought-out programs whose object is to produce a vision or mission for the organization around which more detailed planning and organizing can take place.

I do not intend to discuss these processes at any great length in this chapter. I do think they are the right thing to be focusing on in this period in history when so many organizations have lost their way in the midst of all the turbulence, change, paradox, and contradiction that they face. I have tried to describe elsewhere (see Chapter Three) the reasons organizations have trouble getting clear and staying clear on their mission. I have named the process for doing this *purposing* and have argued that it is the essential leadership quality for achieving high performance. I define purposing as "that continuous stream of actions by an organization's formal leadership that has the effect of inducing clarity, consensus, and commitment regarding the organization's basic purposes." It is my perception that many other writers on leadership have similarly identified this capacity to state the basic direction, chart the course, articulate the vision, as the key quality of the organization leader.

Such statements, though, are about the outer nature of purposing. What we have not been paying enough attention to is the inner side—the personal qualities that make it possible for an individual to engage in these actions called purposing. These qualities are partly matters of sheer intellect and partly matters of having had enough experience with the organization and its environment to see clearly what is needed and what is possible. A way with words, or a speechwriter with a way with words, certainly helps, and an understanding of the psychology of those who have to hear and understand seems to be a crucial element. Knowledge of the technical role a statement of mission or a vision is going to play in the organization's strategic guidance system is important, because otherwise it will not be understood how important follow-through is. The leader has to care about implementation—that is, translating vision into concrete steps.

Millions of training dollars are being spent annually to develop these skills I have named—intellect, experience, verbal charm, insight into others, and knowledge of strategic management processes—and they are unquestionably key qualities. But in my judgment, they are not enough. What is still missing are the core values of the person who would do this thing I am calling purposing. What does the person *care* about? What *matters* to the person? What does the person have genuine, spontaneous, unrehearsed, unmodulated, and unhomogenized energy for? What is at the core of the person's *being*?

To the extent that attempts to state vision and mission and introduce vitality are conducted apart from these basic qualities of the executive's character, the mission will not take hold, the vision will just be an abstract and impersonal dream, and the vitality that is needed to set a complex organizational process in motion will be missing. Instead, fear will be the main engine of vitality. People will do their jobs well enough to avoid getting fired even though they do not know the broader mission and purpose. The implementation process will run on the rails of habit, "the way we did it last year," and the year before that, and the year before that . . .

It is up to the leadership to state with intelligence and conviction the value groundings on which the work of the organization should rest. These value groundings may be a wide variety of different things. For example, they may be the following, singly or in combination: (1) financial goals, (2) quality demands of the task, (3) what is good for the customer or for other stakeholders, (4) what conformity with the law and other ethical standards requires, (5) consistency with past decisions and actions, (6) attainment of the kind of organizational climate members want, or (7) obedience to legitimate higher authority. In other words, one or a combination of the preceding grounds (or others) must be offered persuasively in response to the question, "Why are we doing things the way we are?"

The trouble is, *all* of these kinds of value groundings can be undercut by change, whether the changes are in personnel, in technology, or in markets and other contextual forces. When the grounds of values are undercut, the meaning goes out of the activity. When values are chronically in doubt and adrift in the organization, its operations begin to become literally and profoundly absurd. And when positive reasons cannot be discovered and agreed on for going about things in any particular way, the most basic value of all in the organization has come into question: that the organization's mission is meaningful and valuable, and that the organization should exist to pursue it.

There are millions of executives who *do* care about their organizations, for whom some things *do* matter more than others. I am not primarily making an argument about spiritual emptiness, although for some spiritual emptiness is an issue and has to be considered further. No, it is more often a problem of a *discontinuity* between what the executive is feeling and what kind of person the organization apparently needs as a leader and what kind of contribution that person needs to make. We have so thoroughly technicalized and intellectualized the job of the organization leader that there is no place for the real passions and pains that men and women in these jobs feel. In my experience, more and more of these executives are becoming thoroughly other-directed, that is, preoccupied with how some action on their part will play to the many constituencies who will receive it. It is understandable, but it is tragic because it directs the executive's attention *away* from the very inner qualities that most need to be developed and expressed.

Here, for example, are two mission statements, the first of which was fashioned during a two-day off-site meeting by the top team of a data-processing division in a major, global financial institution:

> To provide responsive automation expertise and cost-effective automated services and facilities to the organization and its clients.

> To excel in providing responsive automation leadership, expertise, and cost-effective automated services and facilities to the organization and its clients.

The first statement was hammered out over two days, and the second emerged in about an hour after the first one was finally crystallized and the team was getting ready to move on. The change was caused by the boss, who was a senior vice president in the parent institution. He had been playing a relatively peerlike role during the workshop. No one had any reason to suspect that he was dissatisfied, but he finally popped. He said he just could not accept the first statement. It had no juice for him, no challenge. He said he had been playing what he called a "participative" role because he did not want to dominate the discussion and he had hoped that an ambitious statement would emerge from the group. But it had not, he said, so he would just have to insist on it himself. He went on to talk intensely about doing the data services job really well, which is what led to the insertion of the term *excel*. Even more important to him was the *leadership* role because, he said, users had little idea what these systems could do. They needed help; they needed education. That was the true function of the group, he insisted, not just reliable number crunching.

It was an impassioned speech by him, not a group discussion. He apologized continually for "dominating." There was no resistance to his ideas but some grumbling about why he had not spoken up sooner, to which he only repeated his fears of dominating.

What impresses me about this situation is how this man's theory about his role, as well as probably some considerable personal shyness and diffidence about expressing strong feelings, almost led him to let his group produce a mission statement that he found boring and inconsistent with his own values and aspirations. I have been in other meetings where it was only learned after the session was over that one or more key people were not at all enthusiastic about what was achieved.

What I think is going on in such cases is what Carl Rogers called "incongruence," and it occurs on a massive scale. Rogers (1961, p. 339) was concerned with the degree of match versus mismatch between three things: a person's total experience of a situation, the parts of it that are allowed into awareness, and what is overtly communicated to others. I think we are possibly in a situation where the real feelings top managers have about themselves, their organizations, and their stakeholders are being systematically suppressed and distorted and ignored in favor of maintaining a front called "executive." Considerable amounts of personal and organizational energy are going into the creation and maintenance of these fronts. It is evident to me, after having sat in many meetings where the boss needed to try to say clearly what he or she really wanted the organization to be, that for many executives the only way to do that is to drop the front and be more real. And it is also evident to me that a considerable number of executives are not letting themselves entertain the possibility of dropping the front, or, if they are thinking about it, they are feeling a lot of anxiety and confusion about it.

It also needs to be said that dropping the front and being more real often makes those around the executive quite anxious themselves. It puts *them* into an environment of novelty and unpredictability that can be very stressful. One senior executive I know in a Fortune 500 firm tried to initiate a series of shirtsleeve, anything-is-fair-game discussions with cohorts of junior managers going through the company's management development program. Only the first two or three meetings were at all candid. A few questions were asked at which the top man became quite testy and even embarrassed. The word quickly went out that these meetings were being held and that there were certain subjects that the boss probably did not want to discuss. Junior managers rehearsed with each other before attending. The bosses of these junior managers gave them questions the bosses wanted asked and named topics that the juniors were not to raise with the top man. In short, what started out as an honest attempt by a senior person to be more real with up-and-coming junior managers turned into a charade. The troops could not handle his testiness and undertook to protect themselves from it.

As hard as it is to be more honest, and as complex as the psychology of the process is, we are in a situation from which there is no turning back. All organizations in Western society, public and private, profit and nonprofit, either are now deep in a process of search for a new mission and purpose or soon will be. And as long as the pace of change continues its chaotic course, the capacity to search and research for basic direction will be the prime element in an organization's survival. It is not an exaggeration to say, therefore, that the deeper springs of leadership energy and commitment are involved in an organization's survival. We have known for decades, even centuries, that the best leaders are able to reach deeply into themselves for inspiration and courage and toughness. This capacity is not just another element on the leadership list. Given what is happening in the world, I think that if we are not talking about these capacities, we are not talking about leadership.

Executive Values and the Statesman Myth

The executive's values are the key thing. This is the basic thrust of the preceding section—that to the extent that a person's values are suppressed or politicized or outright altered to fit some presumed organizational need, he or she will not be able to bring whole-hearted energy and commitment to the task of purposing the organization. I suppose we could try to finesse the problem by arguing that an executive's personal values *should be* those that are appropriate for the organization. If they are not, she or he should not be in the job. But that is a static and mechanistic way of talking. It is mechanistic because it treats values as *things* that can somehow exist in some degree of clear match versus mismatch with each other. While this may be true for such simple questions as whether an individual likes one kind of pie better than another kind, the world of organizational values and value conflicts is a much grayer one where choices are rarely clearly "either this or that." Thus statements about the degree of fit between a person's values and what an organization needs are not so much matters of geometry as, in the currently popular metaphor, matters of chemistry.

Furthermore, to say an executive's values *should* fit the organization's need is static because it assumes that neither the organization nor the person are growing and changing, whereas in fact each is. The problem of fit is created just *because* organizations are trying to stay adaptive in a turbulent environment. The organization may find itself needing to go off in directions its leadership is not interested in or, conversely, the leadership may perceive needs and opportunities it values and wants to pursue that the organization's structure, technology, and culture are not ready for.

By contrast, in a more tranquil and stable world, leaders could become thoroughly acculturated to their organizations and industries. They could settle in for lifelong leadership and service without any thought of encountering a crisis of organizational mission, role, or, indeed, survival. They could contemplate tenures of thirty, forty, and even fifty years of accumulating wisdom and leadership skill in pursuing the basic purposes of the organization, using essentially the qualities of mind, body, and spirit that they had acquired by their late twenties. I call this complex of ideas and experiences the *statesman myth*. It is wonderfully captured in the novels of such writers as J. P. Marquand, C. P. Snow, James Gould Cozzens, and Louis Auchincloss.

This traditional world has now passed, even though the myth lives on in the philosophy underlying most executive development programs. The presumption of these programs is that self-knowledge, self-discovery, and personal growth are not properly part of senior executive education. With very few exceptions, we are tending to treat senior management development as a primarily intellectual process, a matter essentially of knowledge acquisition. We are doing very little to help these men and women take off their masks. We are acting as though the executive position exists secure and ready-made for them, and the only real question is whether they can acquire enough information to govern wisely once they are in place.

The reality today is that we have a much more tenuous relationship between leaders and organizations. We have rapid turnover in the top jobs. We have leaders and organizations getting in and out of phase with each other on basic values and missions. We have organizations having to reinvent themselves and leaders correspondingly going through profound personal transformations, not the least of which involve their physical and mental health and their family relationships. No one ever told the women and men who are living through this period that this was what life at the top levels was going to be like. What they grew up with was the statesman myth, and I suspect that many yearn for a return to that way of being an executive leader.

The most painful part of the collapse of the statesman myth is that it forces a reexamination of values. The capacity to rethink and reexamine basic values is not, to my knowledge, on anyone's present list of key executive abilities. Everybody is talking about paradigm shifts and moving from the industrial to the information age, but few are talking about the qualities of mind, body, and spirit that are involved in executing such shifts, to say nothing of leading others in making the shifts. And few are talking about creating settings in which the men and women we expect to lead organizations can really engage themselves, each other, and the issues at a deep level, a level that brings their spiritual condition into the conversation and provides them with the opportunity to learn and grow spiritually.

The Spiritual Condition of Leaders

It is possibly quite presumptuous to undertake a discussion of the spiritual condition of the women and men who occupy positions of organizational leadership in our society. This topic has not been part of the mainstream of management and leadership theory and research. In a real sense, it is no one's business but the individual's what sort of spiritual condition he or she is in, or at least that is what the norms of Western society say. To talk of another person's spiritual condition can easily become "fightin' words," and Americans tend to believe it is better not to try.

The only response I can make to this norm is that we cannot afford the luxury of silence about the spiritual condition of our leaders. They themselves are experiencing stresses at a deep personal level that many of them cannot cope with, and they are taking actions in their organizations that in many cases reflect their fragile and embattled spiritual condition; thus others are being affected by their spiritual condition. The challenge is to see if we can conduct a discussion of the leader's spiritual condition and spiritual development without either judging or condemning. Both of these are easy modes to fall into, and they probably account for why Americans can be so touchy about the subject of spirituality.

With the phrase *spiritual condition*, I am talking about the feeling individuals have about the fundamental meaning of who they are, what they are doing, and the contributions they are making. I invite you to reflect on this phrase, too. It is one that seems intuitively to mean something significant but that is difficult to pin down very exactly. Of course, the term *spirit* itself is difficult to define exactly, even though many of us would find uses for the word in everyday conversation and would feel when we use it that we mean something that no other word captures quite as well. A moment's reflection will show that we routinely use many phrases with the word *spirit* in them and that for most of these phrases, no other word is quite right for what is intended.

To talk about a spiritual *condition* is to imply that this condition can change, that it is not a fixed characteristic, even though we may not always be able to change our spiritual condition consciously and planfully. Conscious control remains an open question, notwithstanding the enormous literature and body of practice that exists regarding ways to improve one's spiritual condition. *Spiritual* is the really difficult term to be very clear about. Why not use *psychological* or some other word that does not have all the potential for various meanings that *spiritual* does? I use *spiritual* because I think we have to, and here is why.

There are two ways in which a leader is propelled inexorably into the realm of the spiritual. One is in the leader's own desire to act rightly and responsibly. This desire, I suggest, goes beyond the sheer technical correctness of the leader's actions. As a matter of empirical truth, leaders tend not to be satisfied with being merely technically correct. They want to be correct in a way that is consistent with their deeper beliefs about what is important and what the meaning of their life is. I am not saying that a given leader applies this test with equal intensity to all actions; nor am I saying that all leaders exhibit the need to be more than technically correct with equal fervor. I *am* saying that to one degree or another, leaders tend to want to be correct in relation to their values. In this sense, then, *spiritual condition* refers to the degree to which the person acts on values that transcend the sheer material conditions and events of the world, that is, on values that are not contingent for their validity on these conditions and events.

The other way that a leader is propelled into the realm of the spiritual is by having her or his actions scrutinized by other people in terms of their values. The leader's spirit and spirituality are seen through the eyes of others. If the leader is only being technical and materialistic, he or she will be experienced by at least *some* as insufficiently in touch with the deeper things in life. One cannot touch the spirit of others very deeply without coming from the deeper parts of oneself. In this sense, *spiritual condition* refers to the extent to which one is experienced by others as concerned with more than superficial and transitory things.

The one thing I am not claiming is that *spiritual condition* refers to one's degree of closeness to and contact with something otherworldly and divine. For many, spirituality does point in this direction and indeed is specifically concerned with one's experience of the divine. But *spirit* does not have to mean this, and I am willing to let it mean whatever you want in terms of the degree to which it is natural versus supernatural, sacred versus secular. In other words, human beings have found meaningful spirit in all kinds of different places. Where one finds spirit and how one experiences it and is inspired by it vary widely. These differences are part of and reflect one's spiritual condition.

Just as we find inspiring phenomena widely in human experience, so too are there *dispiriting* phenomena—forces and events that seem to take spirit out or that inhibit the experience or apparent action of spirit. Modern organizations can be very dispiriting places, and sadly, they can have dispiriting leaders—leaders whose impact blocks the spirit of others, setting people against each other and souring the climate of the organization.

The presence of dispiriting forces is another reason we can leave the natural versus supernatural question open. We do not have to decide it, *because it does not make any difference whether or not spirit and spirituality deal with the divine*. Human experience shows that the dispiriting forces can eat away at spirit whether we have been seeking it in sacred or secular places. Religious faith is no more immune to temptation and despair than secular faith. The difference between them is not in their degree of immunity, but in the explanations they offer for the source and meaning of spirit. Those *within* religious faith will insist that their faith is stronger and better grounded than the faith of those who are trying to sustain a secular faith, but it also has to be said that religious faith can be sorely tested. Dispiriting events and experiences do not melt away once religious faith is acquired. In short, whatever modes of spirit we are trying to have faith in and stay in touch with, whether sacred or secular, they will be challenged by the dispiriting evils of the world.

The question, then, is not which is right: a sacred faith or a secular faith. The question is what we are able to do, and how we are able to move and develop in our awareness and spiritual condition when the dispiriting experiences occur. We have the opportunity to grow in our faith, to develop in it both as we experience the positive fruits of spirit as we understand it *and* as we are challenged by dispiriting evil. In other words, I am framing the question of spiritual condition and spiritual growth in *process* terms rather than in terms of finally discovering something fixed that one can believe in. Nothing is fixed. The meaning of everything is under assault in this chaotic world. Any equilibrium we achieve will be temporary and dynamic. The spiritual challenge of leadership is to be able to adapt to all these changes without becoming dispirited, for if that happens the danger is that others in the organization will become dispirited, too. The need is to create, maintain, and develop our spiritual condition, and this is why executive development is spiritual development.

Avenues of Spiritual Development

One may ask what is to be worked on as dispiriting experiences are confronted and a deeper sense of spirit is sought. There can be no exact answer to this, since it will vary with the person and with the circumstances. It will also depend heavily on the modes of spirituality an individual is particularly attuned to. The spirit of altruistic service to the poor, the spirit of artistic creativity, and the spirit as the individual finds it in the worship of his or her God may imply quite different experiences and opportunities as the person's spiritual condition unfolds.

However, given that we are talking about men and women who are leaders of organizations, and given that values and human relationships play such an important part, perhaps it is possible to suggest tentatively what some avenues of spiritual development might be for leaders. Furthermore, since leaders are *initiators* of thought and action toward others, the avenues of spiritual development should be matters that can themselves be fostered in the organization. If possible, it would be preferable not to have the leader developing in one direction spiritually while job opportunities and demands are tugging in another direction, because that is a recipe for anger and cynicism.

In much of what I say from now on, you will recognize things that have been said before about what leaders need to be doing. That is as it should be, for I think the subject of spirituality has been implicit in much of leadership theory for some time.

Here are seven fields or modes or contexts of spiritual growth. They overlap and interrelate; they are to be thought of as a system, not a list. They are suggestive rather than definitive, and you are urged to help fill in the picture for each of the seven as well as to critique them and to think of whole new categories. I have not listed the seven in any particular order of importance, except that the one mentioned last is, in my mind, the most important and in some sense it integrates all the others.

1. Toward Embracing New Values and the Possibilities They Imply, and the Relativity of Values to Each Other

Some might call this the evolving ability to see shades of gray rather than only black and white. It might also be called the ability to experience the world hypothetically in "as-if" terms—that is, to imagine other states of affairs than those before us or toward which we have been devoting energy. The behavioral sciences have been calling this process one of moving out of a win-lose frame of mind and toward a win-win mentality.

To some who have not moved out of the either-or mode of judging things, multivalued thinking may look wishy-washy, that is, ready to cave in and accept some atrocious notion at the slightest sign of conflict and pain. The truly democratic spirit that is determined to hear all sides is of course anything but weak; in fact, it is usually tougher than the simplistic, single-valued posture. It has to be tougher! It has more complexity to handle, more disparate imperatives to juggle, more pressure and more stress because it is letting its own values interact with those of others, more reason to throw up its hands and retreat into the black-and-white frame of mind. This is why development of the capacity to practice a democratic style *is* spiritual growth, for a more flexible and resilient spirit is needed to be democratic.

An organization is a place where everybody is right and everybody is wrong. Each person has hold of a piece of the truth; no person has all the truth. Life for the leader in an organization is a process of ongoing discovery of all the ways that various organization members have their truths. Thus, all the talk about a participative style of leadership is superficial to the extent that it does not recognize the spiritual growth that this style entails. In fact, to call this way of being in relation to others a *style* indicates that we have not understood the spiritual demands it places on the person. It is more than a style. Participative management is a way of being, and not something one just adopts after reading a book or sitting through a two-day workshop. "Largeness of spirit" is the quality I am talking about here. The largeness is this capacity to embrace the shades of gray and the many facets of any human situation.

2. Toward a Passionate Reason

Spirituality is wholehearted and wholeheaded, and the more profound it is, the less it resides in any one faculty of the human being and the less it is either mental or emotional, either reasonable or passionate. Spiritual growth is toward a feeling of and a practice of the wholeness of oneself and cannot entail the suppression of one part in favor of another.

I do not think the great philosopher of science Karl Popper (1968) was intending to be spiritual when he settled on the phrase "conjectures and refutations" as the most thorough expression of his philosophy of inquiry and the growth of knowledge. But I think it is a spiritual proposition to say that human beings can proceed only by making the most passionate and daring guesses, hypotheses, and conjectures possible and then attempting to refute them with all the force of their intellectual powers of criticism. To practice either while ignoring the other is to operate at a less than fully human level. Both conjectures and refutations partake of the spiritual, but to grasp that and practice it requires a more profound spiritual condition than to be simply good at either one or the other.

Three qualities that are much desired in organizational life these days are creativity, courage, and leadership. A little reflection will show, I think, that each of these qualities is an example of passionate reason. Creativity is both a primal energy for what is new and different and a cool understanding of what is indeed new and different. Courage blends knowledge of the danger one is in with the determination not to be conquered by fear. Determination and resolve are much more matters of emotion, I believe, than they are logical conclusions. But courage would not be courage if it did not blend rational understanding of the situation with an emotional commitment to hold to a particular course no matter what. And leadership is neither just knowledge of what is needed nor just the desire and willingness to provide what is needed; it is both, bound inextricably together such that neither makes much sense without the other. We try to teach leadership as if its essence can be communicated in theories and research findings, but without the feeling that accompanies the intellectual appreciation of situations, there can be no real leadership. Of course, we can err on the other side, too. If we overemphasize the raw energy of leadership at the expense of stressing how very smart and insightful most effective leaders are, we miss the mark again.

Doubtless many of the qualities we most admire in people are examples of what I am calling "passionate reason." One in particular deserves some further comment. That is the ability to have faith, the ability, in the currently popular (but originally biblical) phrase, to "keep the faith." It is hard for many of us to have faith, to acquire it and to grow in it. The dispiriting forces I was just discussing cut directly into our faith and make us feel wrong or silly or naive or sorrowful. The best defense we have against these assaults lies in the conjoining of head and heart, of intellect and feeling. Faith grounded more in passionate feeling than reason is vulnerable to surprise, to embarrassment, to being discredited. The loss of a faith whose basis was emotion in the first place results in agony and despair. In the extreme, it results in death. Faith grounded more in reason than passionate feeling (which we then call "having reasons") is untested and somewhat oblivious to the intensity of the tests that can be put to it. Faith that is just mainly reasons is curiously dual: the faith is in the correctness of the reasons but it is also in the *adequacy* of the reasons. The reasons for believing what one believes may be quite correct, but they may be quite inadequate relative to the intensity and relentlessness of the challenges that can arise. Intellectual reasons for not sinning are rarely enough, for opportunities to sin can be too tempting. The determination has to go deeper than merely having reasons not to indulge oneself.

The deepening faith that accompanies an improving spiritual condition has to be more and more thoroughly a passionate reason. The process of spiritual growth presents continuing opportunities to err too far into one kind of faith or the other, that is, into a mindless ecstasy or an intellectual labyrinth of nuances and distinctions. Yet if our spirituality is going to remain in the world and engaged with the world's people, its problems, and its objectives, it seems to me that the balance captured in the notion of passionate reason is the best approach.

3. Toward the Development of an Open Value System

Value system is such a common phrase that it is virtually a cliché. However, what it truly means for a set of values to constitute a system is a relatively unexplored notion. The creation of a value system has to be viewed as an achievement, since it means that a person has undertaken a searching comparison of the content of the various values in the system and worked through—both speculatively and, more importantly, in lived experience—the relationships that exist between the values not just as concepts but in concrete action. This means that the various elements of values have been understood not in isolation but as a whole taken together, and that no subsets of values in the value system can be substituted for the whole system without altering its character. Value systems are not lists of values that coexist in the mind of a person, and from which individual values, principles, or guidelines are selected to fit an occasion. Viewed this way, fewer of us than might be thought possess genuine value systems. Possession of a value system is truly a concomitant of spiritual growth and development.

The *openness* of a value system also deserves comment, because the first two avenues I have discussed will surely bring new elements into a value system and cause substantial changes in it. One of the key aspects of openness is the discovery of values deep in another's psyche that we can barely comprehend as values. Openness takes us out of our own value system and into the value systems of others. One of the clearest examples of this is in cross-cultural relationships, where another's values can be so alien and mysterious that they are not even recognized as positive values. I am thinking of common, everyday things like differences in eating habits, differences in the use of time, differences in the significance of material possessions, or differences in the significance of family relationships. The differences can be so great that we cannot believe that the other person's behavior is basically an expression of a different value system; at least we cannot believe it if we are not sufficiently far along in spiritual development. The capacity to experience the *spirit* of another across the cultural gulf is a prerequisite to true intercultural understanding and valuing.

Another type of gulf exists between the various technical specialties that we find in modern organizations. It is common for a specialist in one technology to feel that the spirit of his or her specialty is being denied by the way the other specialties are intruding, in terms of budget, space, influence on broader objectives, attention of key personnel, and so forth. Many, many professionals are throwing up their hands daily because they feel that the organization is crushing the spirit of their specialty or profession. At one level of spiritual awareness and development, spirit may seem to be a win-lose game. This type of spiritual warfare cannot continue, though, for the modern organization needs the spirited practice of all its various special fields of technical competence. Spiritual empowerment is one of the most important kinds of empowerment there can be.

These problems are usually discussed under the rubric of *boundary management*, but without the notion of spirit and spiritual development, boundary management can hardly mean more than merely keeping people out of each other's way. This may be enough in some cases, but most organizations are more than loose coalitions of high-energy teams whose spiritual values and energy are for the most part imploded on their own specific mission.

The various parts of the organization *are* a value system in addition to being a system in structure and in communication. You do not hear it put this way very often—that an organization is a value system—but the more we perceive the action of spirit in an organization, the clearer this becomes. What this says to leaders, therefore, is this: "You are a living value system yourself and you are leading a living value system—your organization. The nature of each of these as well as their relationship will become clearer and clearer to you as your own spirit develops and deepens." Without this avenue of spiritual development, the leader is likely to experience little more than a cacophony of competing priorities and constraints, both inside the self and outside in the organization and the wider environment.

4. Toward Spiritual Development That Is Shared with Others

The discussion of boundaries and of others' value systems in the preceding section suggests another avenue of spiritual development, namely, the growing ability to work on matters of spiritual development with others. The *fellowship* aspect of spiritual development is a very old quality of spiritual growth in many of the world's great religions. One can guess that its significance stems partly from the more practical realization that we may be able to develop more richly and creatively if we have the presence and the support of others who are engaged in a spiritual search with us. Perhaps there is no more significant avenue of spiritual development for organization leaders than this one, because it leads organization members into a fuller realization of their interdependence and of their common feelings, loyalties, opportunities, and strengths. Fellowship helps both leaders and members to confront the loneliness, disappointment, and pain of the modern organization and to decide that these conditions should not continue to rot the spirit of the organization and the people in it.

There is relatively little discussion of organizations as *spiritual families*, although the data that have been accumulating on excellent organizations makes it very clear that this is what these organizations are: spiritual brotherhoods and sisterhoods. What it takes in leadership and membership to move toward spiritual kinship is not well understood in contemporary Western organizations. The literature is small, which makes the appearance of books that do confront the spiritual horror of organizational life all the more significant. Some recent examples are Scott and Hart (1979), Kelly (1988), and Harvey (1996). Harvey in particular makes it crystal-clear that spiritual horror coexists with the potential for spiritual kinship in the modern organization.

It is ironic, even tragic, that we already know in precise detail how to help people move toward a deeply felt conviction of their membership in a spiritual family. The methodology is that of the encounter group, the sensitivity training group, or the T-group; I take all these phrases to mean virtually the same thing. By just asking a group of ten or a dozen people to focus on what is happening right there in the group, it is possible to help group members experience feelings in themselves and others that are not as easy to attend to and learn from in everyday life. Discovery of things in oneself and others that one never knew were there is the hallmark experience of these groups. The discovery is sometimes of dark and frightening things, but much more often it is of tender and beautiful and positive things. I do not think there is any question that these groups produce these experiences, even though they have now become largely passé and tend to be dismissed as one of the kooky things we played with in the 1960s (Vaill, 1985).

To some extent, we misinterpreted what these groups were all about when they were in their heyday. As a result they did not achieve the objectives we thought they should be capable of achieving, and so they passed from prominence in adult learning and development. It is a great tragedy that this happened. What we did not understand, I believe, was that we had invented a fairly modest and nonthreatening setting in which people could experience their spiritual kinship more thoroughly and deeply than many of them ever had before. We tended to downplay this aspect, though, in favor of interpreting these groups as places where technical learning about ourselves and others could go on, where we could learn about communicating effectively, where we could get feedback from others about ourselves in little packets of information that we could then use to improve ourselves. It is as if we thought these groups were primarily places where we could gather a lot of facts about what people are really like and techniques for working effectively with them.

At the same time that we were treating these groups as vehicles for technical learning, we were *evaluating* them, using very technical behavioral science methods, to see whether the technical learning we thought was going on was actually paying off in increased personal effectiveness with people at work. We tried to follow the effects of these groups through to the bottom line. In general, the net of all attempts to prove effectiveness and payoff is about zero. T-groups did not prove out as tools for making people and organizations more effective and efficient. As a result, corporate America tended to lose interest.

There was one research finding that emerged repeatedly in these groups, but not much importance was attached to it per se. In fact, many did not even interpret this constant occurrence as a research finding at all. I refer to the fact that in these groups people talked about things that for the most part they could not and did not talk about anywhere else, and they felt things about themselves and others that for the most part they could not let themselves feel in quite as full and healthy a way in any other place. These groups affected people's spiritual condition, and I think the effect was overwhelmingly positive. Possibly now, twenty years after they peaked in popularity, we are in a better position to see what these groups were really about. And perhaps if we are interested in spiritual development, some of these methods of facilitating human encounters warrant another look.

5. Toward a New Vocabulary and Grammar of Spirituality

We have to talk with ourselves and others if we are going to understand and improve our spiritual condition. The adequacy of the language we have for conducting this talk is itself a matter of growth and change. The vocabulary of Sunday school, augmented by the wisdom of greeting cards, bumper stickers, and T-shirts, may not be quite enough for leaders to conduct these personal and organizational processes.

The two aspects of this issue that I think deserve special attention are the problem of self-consciousness and the problem of prayer. For some, the use of language that deals with spirituality sounds artificial, stilted, and preachy. It is not "cool" in some circles to interpret experience in spiritual terms, and many will err on the side of keeping silent or of rephrasing their ideas in right-sounding psycholinguistics rather than risk being perceived as having "got religion." This, of course, is not true of everyone, and indeed in the late 1980s millions of people *are* exploring the new vocabularies of spirituality, whether from inside or outside an established religion. Still, I think hesitancy to let one's vocabulary become infused (and inspired?) with spiritual language is real and has to be worked through even as the ideas and spiritual feelings behind the words have to be worked through.

One of the interesting things that happens along this avenue is the rediscovery of genuine, here-and-now meaning in words and phrases we have been hearing all our life but not really comprehending. I am referring to phrases that are used at invocations and benedictions, weddings and funerals, the verses of songs and the mottoes and even mission statements that organizations chisel across their facades but then do not look up at often enough.

Along this avenue, the things people say about their basic beliefs take on a deeper meaning. Their personal credos become virtually a call of their spirit. For example, leadership theorist Harlan Cleveland (personal communication, 1987) reports hearing the explorer Thor Heyerdahl say that his personal credo was "translating ideas into events to serve people." Or again, there is Winston Churchill's profound portrayal of himself on becoming prime minister in 1940 (Churchill, 1948, p. 667): "I felt as if I were walking with Destiny, and that all my past life had been but a preparation for this hour and for this trial."

The further one goes into the spirituality in and of language, the more that tried-and-true words like *faith, soul, sin, tragedy, redemption*, and *spirit* itself are heard and felt afresh. It is not too much to say that the rediscovery of the spiritual meaning in these words we have been hearing all our life can powerfully enrich our own spiritual growth.

The spirituality in music and art and other creative forms also comes forth as we reflect on why particular works were created or what the words in a musical work mean. These nonverbal "vocabularies" are limitless sources of spiritual insight if we simply assume that the artist's spirit is present in the work. In my experience, the encounter with an artist's spirit through her or his work can be a powerful factor in one's own development. The occasions on which we feel personally touched by an artist's spirit should be cherished.

The question of prayer is also intimately bound up with the condition of our spiritual vocabulary. While there is no one vocabulary for prayer, our capacity to engage in prayerful action is heavily influenced by the ease with which we can express our spiritual feelings to ourselves and others. The more our vocabulary does not get in the way, the more richly and fully we can engage in what is called prayer.

So much has been written about what prayer is and about how to do it that I am very hesitant even to raise the subject. But if we are talking about improving our spiritual condition, I think we are talking about prayer, among other things. *What if prayer were simply defined as the attempt to improve our conscious contact with the spiritual?* If prayer is just a word for that, then maybe much of what makes so many of us nervous about the word (and the theology within it that we half-consciously think the word will force on us) falls away. Perhaps prayer is nothing more than focusing deliberately on this spiritual stuff, with possibly just one additional qualifier: it seems to me that in prayer we are not standing back and checking out the spiritual; instead, we are immersing our awareness in whatever form of the spiritual is before us. We try to feel *with* Albinoni in his *Adagio*, for example, rather than eye detachedly the sweet sadness he conveys. We listen to a speaker passionately rather than skeptically, seeking to merge our awareness with the other person's rather than standing back to critique it. We try to look *into* the feeling of the writer rather than just stay on the surface of the words.

Spirit is where you find it and spirituality is finding it and embracing it in prayer, I think. William Barrett (1978, p. 281) anticipates our protest that we cannot lead our lives in this mode by quoting Isaac Bashevis Singer: " 'Whenever I am in trouble, I pray. And since I'm always in trouble, I pray a lot. Even when you see me eat and drink, while I do this, I pray.' "

Following this reasoning out to its logical conclusion, the exploration by leaders of these various avenues of spiritual development is *prayer!* It would then be prayer to try to sense more fully the capacity and the potential organization members have for commitment to the mission. It would be prayer to try to understand another person's spirit. It would be prayer to seek to express ourselves as clearly and persuasively as possible. It would be prayer to seek to develop a value *system* that is honest to our own spirit and responsive to the spirit of others. The negative form would be this: actions that avoid or are indifferent to spirit are at least potentially antiprayer. They may diminish conscious contact with spirit. Defined this way, there can be nothing automatic or ritualistic about prayer, even though we may have *forms* of prayer we use repeatedly. Each occasion becomes a new opportunity to develop contact with the spirit in whatever the action is about.

This approach also throws light on why prayer is hard for so many of us. If you think about it, there really should not be anything hard about prayer. It is a private activity with relatively few rules and no apparent costs of failure. Furthermore, prayer by the definition I have given should be quite easy, since what we are doing is dwelling on our contact with the spirit in an object. As we experience the spirit in something, our feelings are joy, eagerness, curiosity, wonder, comfort, relief. These are not feelings that we normally avoid or suffer from, so why should prayer be difficult?

I am afraid the answer is inescapable: too many of us, too much of the time, have committed ourselves to actions that are indifferent to or deny outright the spirit in us that propels the action and the spirit in the people and things toward which we are acting. It is as if we cannot afford to seek the spirit, because this will bring us face-to-face with the wastefulness, emptiness, or destructiveness of much that we do. In the presence of the spirit of the forest, we do not trash the ground. Feeling the spirit in a person's loyalty, we would not preemptively fire him or her. Sensing our own yearning for more authentic contact with those around us, we would not schedule ourselves so tightly that we can engage in no more than superficial pleasantries with any of them. Perceiving the spirit of a person's cherished innovation, we would not tell the person that it will not work. Feeling a sense of comradeship with an attractive colleague beginning to replace the selfish lust we first felt toward that person, we would not then go ahead and hit on her or him anyway.

Yes, I think prayer is hard because of the shift it requires within us. This is perhaps the deepest mode of leadership we can speak of—the decision by a leader to turn toward the spirit in self and in others and begin to try to experience it more fully in prayer. Will this result in greater profits? More efficient attainment of objectives? Better adaptation to the environment? We have no way of knowing. It *will* result in more spiritually grounded action, whatever that turns out to be.

6. Toward Appreciation of the Spirit in Larger and Larger Wholes

Thinking holistically and appreciating the big picture are routinely mentioned as key qualities of the executive leader. What we do not know as much about is just *how* a leader manages to see the big picture, unless it is just by accumulating more and more data and more and more experience and hoping that in rolling these around in his or her mind a larger synthesis will emerge. Data and experience, however, do not automatically yield a synthesizing vision.

The reason it is hard to see the big picture in any collection of people and things is that they are just too miscellaneous and various; there is too much change and confusion and too much clamor from the various parts for attention. Since the person who would grasp the big picture is part of the system, the big picture to be seen is what *we* have in common, what *we* are involved in, what the meaning is of what *we* are doing. We have to include ourselves in the big picture. This is not an abstract intellectual exercise, but instead the act of taking the lead in interpreting for ourselves and others the broader meaning of the group or organization.

Perhaps it is the spirit of the enterprise, whatever it is, that transcends all the miscellany. Perhaps we can first feel the spirit in ourselves and then feel it in reverberation from others. The task is to feel it and articulate the feeling to ourselves and others. The feeling will be faint and equivocal at first and may remain so. But it may not. Possibly as we work to experience it more fully it becomes clearer and stronger and we become more sure of the meaning and value of the activity, and more able, indeed eager, to communicate it to others in acts of spiritual leadership.

The appreciation of the whole is not a once-and-for-all act, because every whole exists within a larger whole. There is no reason why the process I have just described cannot go on indefinitely. Seeing the big picture then becomes instead a progressive process, a process of progressive transcendence of the limits of our understanding and appreciation of what we are involved in. This progressive transcendence is, I think, the spiritual growth I have described. By definition, the spiritual dimension is unlimited in scope. The higher consciousness that has been intuited so often over the centuries may be just this attainment of a scope and richness of appreciation that goes beyond the ordinary.

An organization leader with the usual everyday pressures and responsibilities might well view this process as departing into abstract and ethereal visions of the organization, so far removed from getting work done as to be of no use at all. I think the exact opposite might be the case, and my reason concerns what feeling the spirit of something really amounts to. The experience of the spirit in things brings us into closer touch with the concrete. Grasping the spirit of a factory, for example, permit us to walk through it attending to myriad details, holding multiple simultaneous conversations, asking and answering questions, pausing to be briefed on particular problems, making promises and juggling conflicts, and so on, all the while staying engaged and cheerful about the place. The sense of the spirit of it all is what makes creative immersion in the details possible. Really effective leaders are legendary for their attention to detail and for their tireless involvement with specifics. It is not because their view is narrow and compulsive, I am convinced, but just the opposite: their view is infused with the spirit running through all the specifics. So once again, we come upon spiritual development as indispensable to what we already agree needs to be done—in this case to help leaders grasp the whole or the big picture of the activities and organizations they are involved in.

7. Toward Centering in the Present

At the beginning of this discussion of avenues of spiritual development, I said that this last avenue was the most important one to me and that in many ways it integrates all the others. The main reason is that organizational leadership is so much a matter of our capacity to be effective in the moment of action, and organizational life is so full of distractions that pull us out of the present moment.

Roethlisberger (1954, pp. 3–29) has given an extraordinary account of how effective action in organizations is an ongoing process of balancing in the here-and-now the many conflicting pressures that any manager feels. Genuine skill, for him, could be found in the way the healthy personality is able to pay attention simultaneously to what is going on outside and inside itself. Thoughts and feelings are inside; other people and the events they cause are outside. "Attention" is the meeting of the two, and "experience" is the cumulative effect through time of paying attention. When inside and outside are meeting and affecting each other freely, effectiveness results. When the inside is suppressed in favor of the outside or vice versa, or when we stop paying attention and rely on a preprogrammed formula or otherwise disengage our attention, the danger is that inappropriate action will result.

At about the same time as the Harvard point of view was evolving in the 1930s and 1940s, Gestalt psychology was developing its own notions about being centered in the present and was defining anxiety as primarily a disorder of attention: a depressive preoccupation with the past or obsession about the future. I am taking a minute to link Roethlisberger and other forerunners to the discussion because I do not want the spiritual possibilities of the present to be thought of as just a piece of "new age" trendiness. The ability of a leader to have a lasting effect is an old notion, not just the teaching of the latest guru.

Among modern executive leaders, one of the biggest barriers to experiencing spirit in the present is *workaholism*, or "hurry sickness," as it is also known. This subject is too large to be explored here, but we have to consider the likelihood that the compulsive action patterns the workaholic develops, and all the rationalistic explanations the workaholic develops to defend these patterns, stand squarely between the person and spiritual growth. In terms of Roethlisberger's ideas about balanced attention, my hypothesis is that workaholism is a disorder of attention: it interprets cues indiscriminately as signals that the workaholic must work more hours and more intensely and that everything depends on her or his willingness to make a superhuman effort. The self-exploration that spiritual growth entails is hard for the workaholic to undertake, since such exploration will reveal the extent to which he or she is addicted to the compulsive workaholic patterns.

If we can agree that expressions of human spirit are constantly running through the thoughts, feelings, and actions of human beings, then wherever the leader is, and whatever the leader is doing, the *present moment* is full of spirit. Even when things feel very flat and humdrum, it is unwise to assume that there is no spirit anywhere in the situation or that the other people in the situation are feeling no stirrings of spirit within. *The present is the place where spirit is most naturally found—that is the main point.* There may be set, ceremonial occasions when a more intense and visible outpouring of spirit occurs, but relative to everyday life these ceremonies are artificial and misleading. We have all walked, full of hope, out of some extravagant ceremony where we have seen much excitement and expressions of new commitment, only to find a few days later that things have settled back into a business-as-usual mode. The spirit of the ceremony seems to have evaporated entirely. Not surprisingly, over a period of time we become cynical about the value of ceremonies. But the artificiality of the ceremony is the wrong place to look for spiritual energy. We must look in the normal expressions of the present, because it is from those normal expressions that a more focused and visible outpouring is going to occur if it is going to occur at all.

There is another curious thing about the present, if this is not too mystical an idea. The present is the only door through which the eternal can enter our awareness. "When mating with Heaven," says my favorite translation of the *Tao Te Ching,* "can you take the female part?" (Bynner, 1980, p. 30). We are counseled to open ourselves, to be willing to *receive* the larger truths of life, rather than to believe that we can *wrest* these truths from experience through intense, sustained effort. The "big idea," the "new vision," the "breakthrough"—these kinds of experiences can only come to us in the present. If some management team is so locked on the rails of its plan or the anxieties of its present crisis or is exhausted and without energy to engage the situation in which it finds itself, the new vision for the organization is simply not going to come.

Therefore, all the other avenues of spiritual development come together in this last one. All the things I have talked about are going to be felt and done in the present or they are not going to be done at all.

Conclusion

The main point of this discussion is that it makes no sense to talk about a leader inspiring an organization if the leader's own spiritual condition and spiritual development are not also considered. Such consideration then takes us into the whole subject of spirituality as it applies to men and women in positions of leadership responsibility, and in the process a variety of difficulties and complexities are discovered, not the least of which is the somewhat taboo nature of the subject. It is not necessary to take a position on religion in discussing spirituality, because problems of spiritual growth and development arise whether our interest in spirit is this-worldly or otherworldly. In the final section of the chapter, seven avenues of spiritual development have been discussed. While these seven paths are by no means the only ones, taken together they involve many important aspects of spiritual growth.

Afterword

Toward a Pushy Collegiality

Over the past thirty years or so, a quiet but increasingly intense war has been going on for the soul of the managerial leader. The principal combatants in this war are two, with many fellow travelers on both sides. On one side are those for whom the most interesting thing about the managerial leader is action: the bottom line, managing for results, getting things done, running the show, being a hard-charging, no-nonsense pragmatist. Those are the hall-mark qualities of effective managerial leadership. They are the reason the managerial leader is interesting and significant. They are why business schools and executive development programs exist—to put content and steam into these qualities. The essence—the quintessence—of this way of thinking is the can-do spirit, that frame of mind that Americans are most famous for and of which they are the most proud.

On the other side are those who find the managerial leader interesting because of the complexity of his or her world, the importance of wise action in that world, and the consequences for organizations and society of actions in that world. From this point of view, the managerial leader ought to be primarily a thinker, one with the capacity to reflect deeply on experience, to examine the consequences of various courses of action, to balance the multiple dimensions of any course of action, to be open to feedback, and to be able to engage continually in meaningful dialogue with various stakeholders, no matter how strident or demanding they are. The highest compliment of the supporters of action is to call the leader a "pragmatist"; the highest compliment this side can pay is to call a managerial leader "perceptive" and a "continual learner."

The war is being fought in classrooms and training seminars, in bookstores and the pages of the business press, in performance reviews and commencement speeches. How much time are we going to spend thinking about it before we cut to the chase and do something? (The distinction I am making in this chapter needs to be much more thoroughly documented and developed, and I intend to do that in a future publication. For the moment, you are invited to identify two or three books or schools of thought on both sides of the debate as a context and validity check for my statements.)

Supporters of the managerial leader as pragmatist see the perceptivist style as passive and woolly-minded, prone to overthinking, and too often stalling in paralysis by analysis. Meanwhile the perceptivists (although by definition they should be more understanding and accepting) often are quick to point out how linear and simplistic the pragmatists seem, how they risk tunnel vision as they rush to judgment, how their approach to things can often be best described as "Ready, Fire, Aim!" These conflicting views occur among practicing managers, but they also occur among consultants and academics. A particularly awkward form of the war takes place when a pragmatist practicing manager has to sit and listen to a perceptivist speaker or consultant or, worse yet, has to take a college course for credit from a perceptivist professor. The same situation with the roles reversed can also be quite embarrassing: a pragmatist "expert" often looks shallow and ridiculous to a perceptivist practitioner.

I am deliberately writing rather informally here because I want to convey the pervasiveness of this ongoing battle over how we are to think of the managerial leader. I also want to show that it is too often being fought in terms of clichés and loaded language. Of course, there are all kinds of shades of gray between the two extreme forms I have sketched. But I have heard the extreme forms very frequently, both among managers themselves and among those who theorize about and write about and speak to managers.

You can see the war going on in the pages of this book. The pragmatic spirit is especially evident in Chapters Three, Four, and Five, whereas Chapters Six, Nine, and Ten treat the managerial leader more as a thinker and reflector—someone who muses about and distinguishes between things, rather than just charging ahead with but one thought in mind. Other chapters display different forms of the two points of view, although with the lines not quite so clearly drawn.

The reason I am dwelling on these two broad views of the managerial leader is that I don't think the war can or should continue. We have to find a higher synthesis that both sides can rally around and that can be the basis for new theory, research, and education. In the midst of the truly awesome challenges to managerial leaders, we do not have the luxury of leaving managerial leadership as only hands-on problem solving or only academic navel gazing. In the *real* real world, you can't survive purely as a hands-on problem solver or as a hands-off philosopher.

Especially in what I call the world of permanent white water (see Chapter Six and Vaill, 1989, 1996) the pressures on the combatants are enormous. Having turned their backs on deep reflection, the pragmatists can only swim harder and harder in the ever-increasing turbulence and cascading power of the contemporary organizational world. The pragmatists cling ever more desperately to formulas: the cookbooks, the five easy steps, the total system approaches. The formulas won't do in the maelstrom of change, and everybody knows it. But if you have turned your back on more philosophical reflection in dialogue with others, the formulas and the beguiling speakers who present them, at very high prices, are all you have.

Meanwhile, if you *do* like reflection and dialogue, the roar of the torrents of change can also be disconcerting, but in a different way:

it is all so fascinating, and the theory of change itself needs so much work. Systems thinking, and chaos theory, and complexity theory, and all that other Margaret Wheatley stuff are such intriguing and promising lines of thought, but they require a lot of time to think through and to utilize. Moreover, the simple tasks of an organization—producing products and services, organizing the work, keeping the books—almost aren't grand and momentous enough for these higher modes of thought. The more we focus on these delicious bodies of ideas, the harder it is to see exactly what nitty-gritty actions will work in the white water so that the organization can stay afloat and, perhaps more significantly, the harder it is to stay interested in the mission and the organization's reason for being.

This war, along with its many forms of contemporary escalation, is a tragedy. The truth is that in our challenging and turbulent organizational world we need the best qualities of both sides, synthesized and integrated in the men and women who are becoming managerial leaders. We need men and women who can think about, write about, teach about, and practice what I have come to call "pushy collegiality." This phrase itself joins the two worlds: "pushy" is colloquial, down-to-earth, focused just on what needs to be done, unpretentious, hands-on. "Collegial" has a bit more lofty ring, carrying the suggestion that the *way* we work and the *way* we are with each other is as important as, or even more important than, what we get done together. But neither term will do by itself. We need both. We need the itch to get on with it, to find goals that are meaningful and courses of action that are doable. But we also need the trust and respect that collegiality implies, and we need to be willing to take the time with each other that the creation of trust and respect requires. The practitioner of pushy collegiality can do both things. The writer-conceptualist about pushy collegiality can talk about them together in an integrated way.

The spirit of the joined concepts is mutually enriching: it is through his or her pushiness that a manager finds colleagues in the first place, in the form of fellow team members, fellow pursuers of the goal or the dream. The manager's pushiness infects team members, not by itself but by its collegiality. Pushy collegiality isn't satisfied until the *team* is on board with what one is being pushy about. Members find such a managerial leader fun and stimulating to be with, uplifting to talk to, a pleasure to sign up with for the work the leader wants to do. Likewise, collegiality energizes the pushiness. Collegiality—the warmth, the support, the new ideas—gives the leader something to push *for*, a new focus for her or his passions. One is not usually pushy in a vacuum. One is pushy for, with, and yes, sometimes against others. The pushiness is collegial; the collegiality is pushy.

But there is more to be said about the integration of the two terms, for if it were as easy as I have noted here it would have been achieved long since. So much has been made in this book, as well as by so many others, of the ethical, moral, and spiritual qualities of effective managerial leadership. Pushy collegiality is a view of managerial leadership that makes the ethical, moral, and spiritual real and natural, rather than a kind of awkward add-on to the main content of the role. A commitment *both* to getting the job done *and* to developing deep collegial relations cannot be sustained without ethical and moral consciousness and a commitment to one's own spiritual development. That is the nub of it. That is the insight that has eluded theories of managerial leadership for as long as theorists have been saying that effective leaders give attention to both task and "social," are both effective and efficient, possess both a concern for production and a concern for people. We have yet to find integrative ways of talking about the two dimensions and meanwhile, as I have argued, a war has heated up between the two.

Another way to say this is that the integration of people and productivity is a transcendental problem. The long-sought-for integration does not reside at the same level or in the same terms in which each half is phrased. The integration is not merely rhetorical, it is not merely additive, it is not achieved just by alternating emphasis between the two halves, and I believe it is not to be achieved just by attempting a purely intellectual integration and synthesis. "Pushy collegiality" is paradoxical. It is oxymoronic. (Some people think that an oxymoron is merely a pair of contradictory terms. It is more: it is an unusual juxtaposition of terms that throws new light on the meaning of each term and that also suggests a new truth in their combination.)

I have noted several times that the war between action and reflection, between the pragmatic and the perceptive, exists among all roles that are concerned with the managerial leader. As a closing thought for this book, I would like to suggest a starting place for the transcendental problem of pushy collegiality—two starting places, in fact. First, I believe that I have considerable anecdotal evidence that there already are practicing managerial leaders who are integrating action and reflection, the pragmatic and the perceptive. My hypothesis is that these individuals who are integrating action and reflection are consciously performing the transcendental act I have mentioned: they are consciously conceiving of the organization and the people in it in transcendental terms. The organization is not for them merely a material thing. They are not the prisoners of the material-instrumental model that is debunked with such passion in Chapter Ten. This for the moment is a hypothesis, but I think a very interesting and promising one.

We need to get on with the investigation of this hypothesis, and that leads me to my second closing thought: pushy collegiality applies to investigators every bit as much as it applies to "investigatees." I don't think transcendental thought and action by practitioners can be studied if the investigator is not capable of transcending traditional modes of investigation. Chapter Two talks a lot about this process, and so does Chapter Nine. What I call in Chapter Nine the respiritualizing of the psyche applies to the investigator of pushy collegiality too. This daring and outrageous statement, this suggestion that we know so little about managerial leadership because we have practiced impoverished modes of investigation and in the process have impoverished ourselves, comes to little if we do not take the next step. And, in fact, some serious investigators are beginning to do just that. I don't know what we will find down the road of transcendent research methodology, but I am sure it will be more interesting, useful, and inspiring than what we know at present. We are not the first to envision that road, nor will we be the first to start down it. But perhaps within our local sphere of the contemporary organizational world of permanent white water, we will discover a few things practicing managerial leaders will find worth knowing.

References

Ackoff, R. L. *Redesigning the Future*. New York: Wiley, 1974.

Barfield, O. "The Rediscovery of Meaning." In R. Thruelsen and J. Kobler (eds.), *Adventures of the Mind*. (2nd series.) New York: Vintage Books, 1961.

Barnard, C. *The Functions of the Executive*. Cambridge, Mass.: Harvard University Press, 1938.

Barrett, W. *Time of Need*. New York: HarperCollins, 1972.

Barrett, W. *The Illusion of Technique*. New York: Anchor Books, 1978.

Bridges, W. *Surviving Corporate Transitions*. New York: Doubleday, 1988.

Bynner, W. (trans.) *The Way of Life According to Lao Tzu*. New York: Putnam, 1980. (Originally published 6th century B.C.)

Churchill, W. *The Gathering Storm*. Boston: Houghton Mifflin, 1948.

Cleveland, H. *The Knowledge Executive*. New York: Truman Talley, 1985.

Copeland, M. *And Mark an Era: The Story of the Harvard Business School*. New York: Little, Brown, 1958.

Cox, S. *Indirections*. New York: Viking (Compass Books ed.), 1962.

Deming, W. E. *Out of the Crisis*. Cambridge, Mass.: MIT Center for Advanced Engineering Study, 1986.

Emerson, R. W. "Literary Ethics." In R. E. Spiller (ed.), *The Collected Works of Ralph Waldo Emerson*. Vol. 1. Cambridge, Mass.: Belknap Press of Harvard University Press, 1971. (Originally published 1838.)

Emery, F., and Trist, E. "The Causal Texture of Organizational Environments." *Human Relations*, Feb. 1965.

Etzioni, A. *The Moral Dimension: Toward a New Economics*. New York: Free Press, 1988.

Forester, C. S. *The Indomitable Hornblower*. New York: Little, Brown, n.d. [Compendium of three novels, including *Lord Hornblower*.]

Hartshorne, C. *Reality as Social Process*. New York: Free Press, 1953.

Harvey, J. *The Abilene Paradox and Other Meditations on Management*. San Francisco: Jossey-Bass, 1996.

Heidegger, M. *Sein und Zeit* [Being and Time] (J. Macquarrie and E. Robinson, trans.). New York: HarperCollins, 1962. (Originally published 1927.)

Hunt, J. *The Ascent of Everest*. London: Hodder & Stoughton, 1953.

Hurst, D. "Why Strategic Management Is Bankrupt." *Organizational Dynamics*, 1986, 15(2), 5–27.

Jones, R. S. *Physics as Metaphor*. New York: NAL/Dutton, 1983.

Juran, J. M. *Juran on Planning for Quality*. New York: Free Press, 1988.

Kelly, C. *The Destructive Achiever*. Reading, Mass.: Addison-Wesley, 1988.

Kroc, R. *Grinding It Out*. Washington, D.C.: Regnery, 1977.

Kuhn, T. S. *The Structure of Scientific Revolutions*. Chicago: University of Chicago Press, 1970.

Lawrence, D. H. "Morality and the Novel." In E. D. McDonald (ed.), *Phoenix: The Posthumous Papers of D. H. Lawrence*. New York: Viking Press, 1968. (Originally published 1925.)

Long, N. "The Political Act as an Act of Will." *American Journal of Sociology*, July 1963, 69.

Magnet, M. "Managing by Mystique at Tandem Computers." *Fortune*, June 28, 1982, pp. 84 ff.

Mailer, N. *Of a Fire on the Moon*. New York: Little, Brown, 1970.

Marrow, A. *The Practical Theorist: The Life and Work of Kurt Lewin*. New York: Basic Books, 1969.

Maslow, A. H. *Motivation and Personality*. New York: HarperCollins, 1954.

McGregor, D. *The Human Side of Enterprise*. New York: McGraw-Hill, 1960.

Mintzberg, H. *The Nature of Managerial Work*. New York: HarperCollins, 1973.

Owen, H. *Riding the Tiger*. Potomac, Md.: Abbott, 1991.

Peters, T. J., and Austin, N. *A Passion for Excellence*. New York: Random House, 1985.

Peters, T. J., and Waterman, R. H. *In Search of Excellence*. New York: HarperCollins, 1982.

Popper, K. *Conjectures and Refutations: The Growth of Scientific Knowledge*. New York: HarperCollins, 1968.

Roethlisberger, F. J. *Man-in-Organization*. Cambridge, Mass.: Belknap Press of Harvard University Press, 1968.

Roethlisberger, F. J., and others. *Training for Human Relations*. Boston: Harvard Business School Division of Research, 1954.

Rogers, C. R. *On Becoming a Person*. Boston: Houghton Mifflin, 1961.

Rowe, A. J., Mason, R. O., and Dickel, K. E. *Strategic Management and Business Policy*. Reading, Mass.: Addison-Wesley, 1986.

Scott, W., and Hart, D. *Organizational America*. Boston: Houghton Mifflin, 1979.

Selznick, P. *Leadership in Administration*. New York: HarperCollins, 1957.

Simon, H. *The Sciences of the Artificial*. (2nd ed.) Cambridge, Mass.: MIT Press, 1981.

Steinbeck, J., and Ricketts, E. *Sea of Cortez*. Mamaroneck, N.Y.: P.O. Appeal Press, 1971.

Trist, E. L. "Urban North America: The Challenge of the Next Thirty Years." In W. Schmidt (ed.), *Organizational Frontiers and Human Values*. Belmont, Calif.: Wadsworth, 1970.

Tumin, M. "Business as a Social System." *Behavioral Science*, 1964, 9, 127.

Vaill, P. B. "Management as a Performing Art." Unpublished commencement address, George Washington University, Washington, D.C., May 1974.

Vaill, P. B. "Toward a Behavioral Description of High-Performing Systems." In M. W. McCall, Jr., and M. M. Lombardo (eds.), *Leadership: Where Else Can We Go?* Durham, N.C.: Duke University Press, 1978. Republished by the Center for Creative Leadership, Greensboro, N.C.

Vaill, P. B. "Cookbooks, Auctions, and Claptrap Cocoons." *Exchange: The Organizational Behavior Teaching Journal*, 1979, 4(1), 3–6. (Now the *Journal of Management Education*.)

Vaill, P. B. "OD as a Scientific Revolution." In D. D. Warrick (ed.), *Current Developments in Organization Development*. Glenview, Ill.: Scott, Foresman, 1984.

Vaill, P. B. "Integrating the Diverse Directions of the Behavioral Sciences." In R. Tannenbaum, N. Margulies, F. Massarik, and Associates, *Human Systems Development: New Perspectives on People and Organizations*. San Francisco: Jossey-Bass, 1985.

Vaill, P. B. *Managing as a Performing Art: New Ideas for a World of Chaotic Change*. San Francisco: Jossey-Bass, 1989.

Vaill, P. B. *Learning as a Way of Being: Strategies for Survival in a World of Permanent White Water*. San Francisco: Jossey-Bass, 1996.

Vaill, P. B. "The Unspeakable Texture of Process Wisdom." In S. Srivastva and D. L. Cooperrider (eds.), *Organizational Wisdom and Courage*. Jossey-Bass, 1998.

Weick, K. *The Social Psychology of Organizing*. Reading, Mass.: Addison-Wesley, 1969.

Weisbord, M. R. *Productive Workplaces: Organizing and Managing for Dignity, Meaning, and Community*. San Francisco: Jossey-Bass, 1987.

Young, J. Z. *Doubt and Certainty in Science*. New York: Galaxy Books of Oxford University Press, 1960.

Index